HISTORY OF THE ROMAN EMPIRE

HERODIAN OF ANTIOCH'S

HISTORY OF THE ROMAN EMPIRE

FROM THE DEATH OF
MARCUS AURELIUS TO THE ACCESSION
OF GORDIAN III

TRANSLATED FROM THE GREEK BY
EDWARD C. ECHOLS

UNIVERSITY OF CALIFORNIA PRESS
BERKELEY & LOS ANGELES
MCMLXI

UNIVERSITY OF CALIFORNIA PRESS
BERKELEY AND LOS ANGELES

CAMBRIDGE UNIVERSITY PRESS
LONDON, ENGLAND

© 1961 BY
THE REGENTS OF THE UNIVERSITY OF CALIFORNIA

PUBLISHED WITH THE ASSISTANCE OF A GRANT
FROM THE FORD FOUNDATION

LIBRARY OF CONGRESS CATALOG CARD NO.: 61-6218

DESIGNED BY ADRIAN WILSON

Book vignettes reproduced from wood engravings by
F. W. Fairholt, F.S.A., in S. W. Stevenson, F.S.A.,
A Dictionary of Roman Coins (1889).

TO MY WIFE
MARY VIRGINIA HATHAWAY ECHOLS

ACKNOWLEDGMENTS

I AM grateful to Dr. Linton C. Stevens, Professor of Romance Languages in the University of Alabama, for helpful criticism in regard to style and clarity. I have also to thank Professor Mason Hammond of Harvard University for his encouragement. And I wish to express my appreciation to Miss Genevieve Rogers, of the University of California Press, who assisted greatly in bringing the work to its final form.

The successful completion of this work owes much to the generous and sustained support of the University Research Committee of the University of Alabama. Grants-in-aid enabled me to give full time to the work of translation during two summers, and, even more important, made it possible for me to have access to a library with facilities adequate for the specialized requirements of this project.

For the shortcomings of the work I assume full responsibility.

EDWARD C. ECHOLS

CONTENTS

INTRODUCTION
1

SELECTED BIBLIOGRAPHY
10

BOOK ONE
MARCUS AURELIUS AND COMMODUS
11

BOOK TWO
PERTINAX, DIDIUS JULIANUS
43

BOOK THREE
SEPTIMIUS SEVERUS
77

BOOK FOUR
CARACALLA
109

BOOK FIVE
MACRINUS, ELAGABALUS
135

BOOK SIX
SEVERUS ALEXANDER
153

BOOK SEVEN
MAXIMINUS AND THE GORDIANS
172

BOOK EIGHT
MAXIMUS AND BALBINUS
197

INDEX
215

LIST OF EMPERORS
180–238

MARCUS AURELIUS	161–180
COMMODUS	180–193
PERTINAX	193
DIDIUS JULIANUS	193
SEPTIMIUS SEVERUS	193–211
CARACALLA	211–217
GETA	211–212
MACRINUS	217–218
ELAGABALUS	218–222
SEVERUS ALEXANDER	222–235
MAXIMINUS	238
GORDIAN I	238
GORDIAN II	238
BALBINUS	238
PUPIENUS MAXIMUS	238
GORDIAN III	238–244

INTRODUCTION

THE Roman historians inherited from the Greeks a long and distinguished historical tradition. It was Hecataeus of Miletus who, in the fifth century B.C., first turned rational attention to the skeletal contemporary sources of history—the traditional myths, uncritically accepted, and the local annalistic records, uncritically evaluated. By the beginning of the Hellenistic period, Greek historiography included every form of historical writing: the discursive, rambling accounts deriving from Herodotus; the objective, scientific, and highly literate histories in the manner of Thucydides; partisan histories designed as propaganda; and historical biographies. Men of action described their personal exploits, and histories written to entertain or shock foreshadowed historical fiction. By the end of the fourth century B.C., history was a legitimate and accepted field of literary inquiry.

The Greek writers of the third century B.C., however, failed to find at home a subject worthy of their talents. The growing importance of Rome tended to counteract the decline of Greek influence, and Timaeus of Sicily, in the third century, wrote at some length of his neighbor in Italy. For the next several centuries, great events tended to produce great historians, and virtually every phase of Rome's history was carefully studied and competently published.

The early Roman historians were Greeks. The intent of these writers was to interpret for the Greek-reading world the phenomenon of Rome's rise to a position of dominance in the Mediterranean world. Greatest of these pioneer Graeco-Roman historians was the soldier-statesman-author Polybius

INTRODUCTION

(*ca.* 203–*ca.* 120 B.C.), who wrote a *Universal History* covering events from 220 to 144 B.C. He describes in admirable detail, and with an equally admirable grasp of the issues involved, Rome's familiar extern wars during this important formative period. A pragmatic historian, describing contemporary times, Polybius was a competent analyst and interpreter.

These pragmatic histories, describing in detail short periods of time, were soon replaced at Rome by the annalistic reconstruction of Rome's early history; the formulation of an annalistic tradition was necessitated by the growth of nationalism resulting from Rome's increasing importance in the Mediterranean world. Once the native Roman historiography was firmly established, it soon embraced all the extant historico-literary forms; by the Augustan Age, Latin historians were writing antiquarian history, contemporary history, military history, "literary" history, and the historical biography.

The Graeco-Roman historians continued to write after the field was dominated by the Latin historians. Before the last century of the Republic, the great Stoic philosopher-historian, Posidonius of Apamaea, wrote a continuation of Polybius' *Universal History* covering the period from 144 B.C. to the dictatorship of Sulla. Posidonius, who had visited Rome and had been the teacher of many distinguished Romans at Rhodes, profoundly affected the literary careers of such Roman historians as Livy, Sallust, Julius Caesar, Tacitus, and Plutarch. Indeed, Posidonius has been credited with paving the way for the glory of the Augustan Age by awaking Rome's historians to a realization of her past and future greatness.

The Greek writers of Roman history were still active in the early empire. Dionysius of Halicarnassus wrote a rhetori-

INTRODUCTION

cal account of Rome's origins, and Flavius Josephus produced in Greek an all-inclusive history of the Jews, as well as an eyewitness account of the Flavian conquest of Palestine in A.D. 68–70.

The growing importance of the individual in the empire raised historical biography to a position of major importance. In the first century B.C., Cornelius Nepos wrote his *De Viris Illustribus,* a series of comparative biographies of Greeks and Romans. Plutarch (*ca.* A.D. 46–*post* 120) continued this literary form in a lengthy series of biographies comparing ancient and contemporary figures. Balancing these "antiquarian" biographies are the imperial biographies of Suetonius (A.D. 69–*ca.* 140), in which he described the empire in terms of its chief personalities, beginning with Julius Caesar.

Paralleling the increasing emphasis upon the place of the individual in history was the trend toward epitomes, eclectic and excerpted accounts concerned with long periods of time. Among the most successful of the annalistic epitomizers was the Bithynian, Dio Cassius, who, in the third century of the Christian era, wrote in Greek his history of Rome from 753 B.C. to A.D. 229. Dio's history is the major source of information for much of the post-Flavian period, when Rome's historical *felicitas* at last began to fail. The late historical summarizers, Aurelius Victor, Eutropius, Festus, Zosimus, and others, treat this period briefly in their epitomes.

The imperial biographers of the *Historia Augusta,* which seems to date from the late fourth century, provide information about the emperors from Hadrian through Numerianus in 284.

The third original source for the history of this period of the Roman empire is the *Ab Excessu Divi Marci* by Herodian of Syria, who wrote in Greek an account of the Roman empire from the death of Marcus Aurelius in 180 to the acces-

INTRODUCTION

sion of Gordian III in 238. Dio and Herodian provide the only extant contemporary histories of this important period of the empire.

Iam pridem Syrus in Tiberim defluxit Orontes.
—JUVENAL *Sat. III* 62

When Juvenal was moved to this peevish observation in the second century of the Christian era, the influx of Syria and Syrians into Rome was a recognized and often-deplored fact. Not all second-century Syrians in Rome, however, could be identified with Juvenal's light entertainers. In the field of history, Posidonius of Apamaea made an important contribution in the first century B.C. In the field of government, the Syrian phase began about 186, when the commander of a legion in Syria married the daughter of a priest of Elagabalus in Emesa. When Septimius Severus became emperor in 193, Rome had a Syrian empress, Julia Domna. When Caracalla became emperor in 211, Rome had a half-Syrian emperor; when Elagabalus became emperor in 218, Rome had a Syrian emperor.

The key figure in Rome's Syrian dynasty was Julia Domna. A shrewd, highly capable woman, she had assumed imperial responsibility with her husband. When Caracalla became sole emperor, Julia was put in charge of imperial correspondence and state records. She soon gathered about her the most distinguished literary men of the day, many of whom held important political posts: the jurists Papinian and Ulpian, the biographer Diogenes Laertius, the sophist Philostratus, the historian Dio Cassius.

After Julia's death, she was replaced at court by her younger sister, Julia Maesa. Rich and wily, Maesa plotted the overthrow of Macrinus and placed upon the throne her grandson Elagabalus, the first Syrian emperor of Rome. The Syrian domination was continued by the thirteen-year reign

INTRODUCTION

of Alexander Severus, with whom the dynasty came to an end in 235.

Thus, throughout most of the sixty-year period covered by Herodian's history, Rome was under some degree of Syrian domination. Herodian states that he had a career in the imperial civil service (1.2.5) which enabled him to write much of his history from personal experience and observation. Since his book ends with the year 238, it is hardly likely that he began his career before the accession of Septimius Severus. Marcus Aurelius had no reason to favor Syria, which had supported the unsuccessful pretender Avidius Cassius in 175. Commodus also seems to have taken relatively little interest in the country. But with the accession of Severus and Julia Domna, the time was favorable for an influx of Syrians into the civil service. Severus did not trust the native Romans, since he dismissed the Praetorian Guard and replaced it by veterans from his legions. The Syrian (?) Papinianus served as praetorian prefect under Severus. The imperial bias after 193 was definitely Eastern, and the literary language of the contemporary literary figures was Greek.

Herodian belonged to the educated class in a country where Aramaic was still the spoken language. An educated Syrian would obviously be of value in the records division of the imperial civil service. It may be suggested that Herodian, a trilingual Syrian (Latin sources were employed for the first four books of his history), joined the civil service after the defeat of Niger by Severus.

Herodian's early association with the Syrian dynasty at Rome would account for the amazing "Romanness" of his outlook. Herodian is so thoroughly patriotic and so Romanized that he can speak of his fellow non-Romans as barbarians, and can offer an analysis of his fellow Syrians that is thoroughly unflattering.

Assuming that he began his imperial service with Sep-

INTRODUCTION

timius Severus and ended it under Alexander or soon thereafter, Herodian may have been a member of Julia Domna's Eastern-oriented literary coterie. He read Dio Cassius; he used his sources; it is entirely possible that he knew Dio Cassius. In view of Dio's advanced age in 229, Herodian probably survived his greater contemporary.

Dio had already produced the definitive "world" history of his age. If Herodian, after his long career in letters, had any serious historical intent, an epitome was obviously out of the question. I hazard the guess that the *Ab Excessu Divi Marci* is a true "memoir," but that Herodian had played so minor a role in the period he undertakes to describe from personal observation and experience that he was forced to supplement his limited knowledge by reference to the standard sources. His work therefore does not compete with that of Dio Cassius; instead, he offers a moralizing account of the downward spiral of the empire. We must credit Herodian with enough sense of history to recognize that the death of Marcus Aurelius signified the end of an era. Herodian's chief concern is with the corruption that accompanied the decline in Rome's world position. That he was not a professional historian is apparent. That he was literate, concerned with the recording of history, aware of the long tradition of Greek historiography but at the same time very much a product of his own age, is equally apparent. He is a rhetorician, pompous, repetitive, and derivative. His fabricated speeches in the Thucydidean mode, which were intended to enliven the narrative, generally have the opposite effect. His insight into causes and motivation is superficial and unconvincing; he obviously lacked the personal experience and broad background that are needed for passing judgment on men and events. Perhaps Polybius is right: only the man of action can write history. Herodian's biographical approach to this period of imperial history is not too successful; his

INTRODUCTION

men on all levels are given a curious sameness of character that reminds us of Cornelius Nepos; with Nepos, the career of one Greek general is very much like that of any other Greek general.

Herodian has been criticized for his many sins of omission, among them his failure to note Caracalla's extension of citizenship throughout the empire. We can only suggest that this action of the emperor's was not nearly so impressive at the time as it now seems. Herodian's geography is vague and must be cited with extreme care. His indefinite and inexact data suggest again the narrow limits of his personal knowledge. His decision to ignore the sexual experiments of many of the emperors is odd in the extreme. These clinical observations were basic features of imperial biography beginning with Suetonius, and the general historians, including Dio Cassius, did not overlook them. Herodian was doubtless a sincere moralizer; a Syrian, he would be reluctant to reveal the more spectacular activities of the Syrian emperors.

As a historian, then, Herodian is an amateur; as a stylist he is typical third-century baroque. If he is no Polybius, no Livy, no Tacitus, it is only fair to point out that neither is any other third-century Roman historian. Herodian is a product of his age, and his work is an interesting and valuable specimen of later classical historiography from a period in which original sources are scarce.

The manuscript tradition is discussed in the preface of the Teubner edition (1883) by K. Mendelssohn, and summarized in the Teubner edition (1922) by K. Stavenhagen. They conclude that there are five codices, one from the eleventh century and four from the fifteenth century. A sixth codex, used by Aldus for the *editio princeps* in 1503, has been lost. Three of these fifteenth-century codices derive from one source; the other three, including the lost codex of Aldus,

INTRODUCTION

are from a second source. These two sources derive in turn from a single source which goes back to the archtype. This archtype is also the source of the excerpts quoted by the seventh-century John of Antioch; these excerpts are outside the surviving manuscripts. I have seen none of these codices.

During the Renaissance, Herodian was studied with interest. At the request of Pope Innocent VIII, the Italian humanist Politian prepared, in 1487, and published both at Bologna and Rome, in 1493, so excellent a Latin version of Herodian that it was believed by many to be an original history in Latin. This translation was reprinted with the Greek text many times in the next two centuries.

The first translation into English, prepared from the Latin of Politian by Nicholas Smyth, was published in London perhaps in 1550. Another English translation, by J. Maxwell, appeared in London in 1629 and 1635. G. B. Stapylton produced a metrical version in English in 1652. The last translation into English is apparently that of J. Hart, London, 1749. The first translation into French seems to have been that of Jean Collin in 1541; Léon Halévy was responsible for the second French version of Herodian in 1824, republished in 1860. Adolph Stahr did a German translation in 1858.

Present-day scholarship has been concerned chiefly with Herodian's contributions to a knowledge of individual emperors. The most recent extensive work is the Princeton dissertation of Reynold Burrows, which considers Herodian and Septimius Severus. Twentieth-century classical and historical scholarship has neglected Herodian. This neglect reflects the general indifference of scholars to the period of the late Roman empire. Only a revival of interest in this significant era will lead to an adequate reappraisal of Herodian as a basic source for the eventful and important years treated in his history.

INTRODUCTION

I have based my translation directly upon the Greek text edited by K. Stavenhagen for the Teubner Series (Leipzig, 1922), supplemented by the Latin version of Politian in the edition of 1532, and I had access also to the translations of Hart, Halévy, and Stahr. A variant of the old dictum frequently applies: "Four translators, four versions." I have elected to avoid a slavish adherence to the Greek idiom and style, and have essayed a version for readers without Greek. For readers of Greek I sincerely recommend the Stavenhagen text in the Teubner Series.

For place names I have chosen to employ the Latin versions: for example, Perennis for Perennius. On occasion I have substituted familiar modern place names for the classical forms: for example, Danube for Ister. The names by which the emperors are generally known have sometimes been substituted for those used by Herodian: for example, Elagabalus for Antoninus.

SELECTED BIBLIOGRAPHY

EDITIONS

Aldine. Venice, 1503.
Bekker, I. Leipzig, 1855.
La Roche, J. Vienna, 1863.
Mendelssohn, L. Leipzig, 1883.
Stavenhagen, K. Leipzig, 1922.

TRANSLATIONS

Latin: A. Politianus. Bologna and Rome, 1493.
English: J. Hart. London, 1749.
French: Jean Collin. *L'Histoire de Herodien...*, tournée de grecq en latin par Ange Politian et de latin en francays par Johan Collin. Paris, 1541; 2d ed., Lyons, 1546.
L. Halévy. Paris, 1824, 1860.
German: A. Stahr. Stuttgart, 1858.

BOOKS AND ARTICLES

Baaz, E. *De Herodiani fontibus et auctoritate.* Berlin, 1909.
Dändliker, C. "Die drei letzten Bücher Herodians," *Untersuchungen zur römischen Kaisergeschichte.* Leipzig, 1870. III, 203-320.
Fuchs, K. "Beiträge zur Kritik der ersten drei Bücher Herodians," *Wiener Studien,* XVII (1896), 222-252.
—— "Beiträge zur Kritik Herodians (IV-VIII Buch)," *Wiener Studien,* XVIII (1897), 180-234.
Kettler, G. *Nonnullae ad Herodianum rerum Romanarum scriptorem annotationes.* Erlangen, 1882.
Kreutzer, J. *De Herodiano rerum Romanarum scriptore.* Bonn, 1881.
Pasoli, A. *L'Uso di Erodiano nella vita Maximini.* Milan, 1927.
Roos, A. G. "Herodian's Method of Composition," *Journal of Roman Studies,* V [part 2] (1915), 191-202.
Smits, J. C. P. *De geschiedschrijver Herodianus en zijn bronnen.* Leiden, 1913.

BOOK ONE

MARCUS AURELIUS AND COMMODUS

CHAPTER I

THE majority of writers who have devoted themselves to compiling histories and to reviving the memory of past events have had in mind the eternal glory of learning. They feared too that if they remained silent they might be numbered among the countless hordes of the obscure. Such writers are little concerned with truth in their narratives, however, but pay particular attention to phrasing and euphony, since they are confident that even if their writings have no basis in fact, they will still win a hearing, and the accuracy of their research will not be challenged.

Indeed, some writers, because they abhor tyrants and wish to flatter or honor rulers, countries, and individuals, have lent sparkle to trivial and unimportant events by the brilliance of their words rather than by the clear light of truth. Unwilling to accept from others hearsay evidence and unsubstantiated information, I have collected, in my history, material that is still fresh in the minds of my intended readers;

BOOK ONE

nor do I think that knowledge of the many important events that occurred in a brief span of time will fail to bring pleasure to future readers. If we were to compare this period with all the time that has elapsed since the Augustan Age, when the Roman Republic became an aristocracy, we would not find, in that span of almost two hundred years down to the time of Marcus Aurelius, imperial successions following so closely; the varied fortunes of war, both civil and foreign; the national uprisings and destructions of cities, both in the empire and in many barbarian lands. We would not find the earthquakes, the pollutions of the air, or the incredible careers of tyrants and emperors. Some of these rulers retained their power for a long time; others more briefly. There were even some who, having attained the imperial power and enjoyed the imperial honors for no more than a single day, were immediately killed. Since, in a period of sixty years, the Roman imperial power was held by more emperors than would seem possible in so short a time, many strange and wonderful events took place. The emperors who were advanced in years governed themselves and their subjects commendably, because of their greater practical experience, but the younger emperors lived recklessly and introduced many innovations. As might have been expected, the disparities in age and authority inevitably resulted in variations in imperial behavior. How each of these events occurred, I shall now relate in detail, in order of time and emperors.

CHAPTER II

THE emperor Marcus Aurelius had a number of daughters but only two sons. One of them (his name was Verissimus) died very young; the surviving son, Commodus, his father reared with great care, summoning to Rome from all over the empire men renowned for learning in their own countries. He paid these scholars large fees to live in Rome and supervise his son's education. When his daughters came of age, he married them to the most distinguished of the senators, selecting his sons-in-law not from the aristocrats, with their excessive pride in their ancestry, nor from the wealthy, with their protective shield of riches; he preferred men who were modest in manner and moderate in their way of life, for he considered these virtues to be the only fit and enduring possessions of the soul.

He was concerned with all aspects of excellence, and in his love of ancient literature he was second to no man, Roman or Greek; this is evident from all his sayings and writings which have come down to us.[1] To his subjects he revealed himself as a mild and moderate emperor; he gave audience to those who asked for it and forbade his bodyguard to drive off those who happened to meet him. Alone of the emperors, he gave proof of his learning not by mere words or knowledge of philosophical doctrines but by his blameless character and temperate way of life. His reign thus produced a very large number of intelligent men, for subjects like to imitate the example set by their ruler.

Many capable men have already recorded the courageous and moderate enterprises, marked by both political and military excellence, which he undertook against the barbarian nations to the North and in the East; but the events which, after the death of Marcus, I saw and heard in my lifetime—things of which I had personal experience in my imperial or civil service—these I have recorded.

CHAPTER III

WHEN Marcus was an old man, exhausted not only by age but also by labors and cares, he suffered a serious illness while visiting the Pannonians.[2] When the emperor

---

[1] *The Meditations of Marcus Aurelius,* available in many editions and translations.
[2] Regularly "Paeonians" in the Greek authors.

BOOK ONE

suspected that there was little hope of his recovery, and realized that his son would become emperor while still very young, he was afraid that the undisciplined youth, deprived of parental advice, might neglect his excellent studies and good habits and turn to drinking and debauchery (for the minds of the young, prone to pleasures, are turned very easily from the virtues of education) when he had absolute and unrestrained power. This learned man was disturbed also by the memory of those who had become sole rulers in their youth. The Sicilian despot Dionysus, in his excessive licentiousness, had sought out new pleasures and paid the highest prices for them. The arrogance and violence of Alexander's successors against their subject peoples had brought disgrace upon his empire. Ptolemy, too, contrary to the laws of the Macedonians and Greeks, went so far as to marry his own sister.[3] Antigonus had imitated Dionysus in every way, even wearing a crown of ivy instead of the Macedonian hat or the diadem, and carrying the thyrsus instead of a scepter. Marcus was even more distressed when he recalled events of recent date. Nero had capped his crimes by murdering his mother and had made himself ridiculous in the eyes of the people. The exploits of Domitian, as well, were marked by excessive savagery. When he recalled such spectacles of despotism as these, he was apprehensive and anticipated evil events. Then, too, the Germans on the border gave him much cause for anxiety. He had not yet forced all these tribes to submit; some he had won to an alliance by persuasion; others he had conquered by force of arms. There were some who, although they had broken their pact with him, had returned to the alliance temporarily because of the fear occasioned by the presence of so great an emperor. He suspected

---

[3] Berenice I was actually the stepsister of Ptolemy I (*ca.* 367–282 B.C.). She became his legal wife in accord with the customary Egyptian practice of marriage between brother and sister in the royal family.

that, contemptuous of his son's youth, they would launch an assault upon him; for the barbarian is ever eager to revolt on any pretext.

CHAPTER IV

TROUBLED by these thoughts, Marcus summoned his friends and kinsmen. Placing his son beside him and raising himself up a little on his couch, he began to speak to them as follows:

"That you are distressed to see me in this condition is hardly surprising. It is natural for men to pity the sufferings of their fellow men, and the misfortunes that occur before their very eyes arouse even greater compassion. I think, however, that an even stronger bond of affection exists between you and me; in return for the favors I have done you, I have a reasonable right to expect your reciprocal good will. And now is the proper time for me to discover that not in vain have I showered honor and esteem upon you for so long, and for you to return the favor by showing that you are not unmindful of the benefits you have received from me. Here is my son, whom you yourselves have educated, approaching the prime of youth and, as it were, in need of pilots for the stormy seas ahead. I fear that he, tossed to and fro by his lack of knowledge of what he needs to know, may be dashed to pieces on the rocks of evil practices. You, therefore, together take my place as his father, looking after him and giving him wise counsel. No amount of money is large enough to compensate for a tyrant's excesses, nor is the protection of his bodyguards enough to shield the ruler who does not possess the good will of his subjects. The ruler who emplants in the hearts of his subjects not fear resulting from cruelty, but love occasioned by kindness, is most likely to complete his reign safely. For it is not those who submit from

BOOK ONE

necessity but those who are persuaded to obedience who continue to serve and to suffer without suspicion and without pretense of flattery. And they never rebel unless they are driven to it by violence and arrogance. When a man holds absolute power, it is difficult for him to control his desires. But if you give my son proper advice in such matters and constantly remind him of what he has heard here, you will make him the best of emperors for yourselves and for all, and you will be paying the greatest tribute to my memory. Only in this way can you make my memory immortal."

At this point Marcus suffered a severe fainting spell and sank back on his couch, exhausted by weakness and worry. All who were present pitied him, and some cried out in their grief, unable to control themselves. After living another night and day, Marcus died,[4] leaving to men of his own time a legacy of regret; to future ages, an eternal memorial of excellence. When the news of his death was made public, the whole army in Pannonia and the common people as well were grief-stricken; indeed, no one in the Roman empire received the report without weeping. All cried out in a swelling chorus, calling him "Kind Father," "Noble Emperor," "Brave General," and "Wise, Moderate Ruler," and every man spoke the truth.

CHAPTER V

DURING the next few days Commodus' advisers kept him busy with his father's funeral rites; then they thought it advisable to bring the youth into the camp to address the troops and, by distributing money to them—the usual practice of those who succeed to the throne—to win the support of the army. Accordingly, all the soldiers were ordered to proceed to the assembly field to welcome them. After performing the imperial sacrifices, Commodus, sur-

[4] March 17, 180.

MARCUS AURELIUS AND COMMODUS

rounded by the advisers appointed by his father (and there were many learned men among them), mounted the high platform erected for him in the middle of the camp and spoke as follows:

"I am fully persuaded that you share in my grief over what has occurred, and that you are no less distressed by it than I. At no time when my father was with me did I see fit to play the despot with you. He took greater delight, I am convinced, in calling me 'fellow soldier' than in calling me 'son,' for he considered the latter a title bestowed by Nature, the former, a partnership based on excellence. While I was still an infant he often brought me to you and placed me in your arms, a pledge of the trust he had in you. And for that reason I have every hope that I shall enjoy your universal good will, since I am indebted to you old soldiers for rearing me, and I may properly call you young soldiers my fellow students in deeds of arms, for my father loved us all and taught us every good thing. To follow him, Fortune has given the empire not to an adopted successor but to me. The prestige of those who reigned before me was increased by the empire, which they received as an additional honor, but I alone was born for you in the imperial palace. I never knew the touch of common cloth. The purple received me as I came forth into the world, and the sun shone down on me, man and emperor, at the same moment. And if you consider the matter properly, you will honor me as an emperor born to you, not presented to you. Assuredly, my father has gone up to heaven, where he is already companion and counselor of the gods. But it is our task to devote ourselves to human affairs and to the administration of earthly matters. To set these affairs in order and make them secure is for you to undertake, if with resolute courage you would finish what is left of the war and carry forward to the northern seas[5] the boundaries of the Roman empire. These exploits will

---
[5] I.e., to the North and Baltic seas.

BOOK ONE

indeed bring you renown, and in this way you will pay fitting respect to the memory of our mutual father. You may be sure that he hears and sees what we do. And we may count ourselves fortunate to have such a man as a witness when we do what has to be done. Up to now, all that you have courageously accomplished is attributable to his wisdom and his generalship. But now, whatever zeal you display in further exploits under me, your new emperor, will gain for you a reputation for praiseworthy loyalty and bravery. By these dauntless exploits you will confer upon us added dignity. Crushed at the beginning of a new imperial reign, the barbarian will not be so bold to act at the present, scorning our youth, and will be cautious and fearful in the future, mindful of what he has suffered."

After he had finished his speech, Commodus won the support of the army by a generous distribution of money and returned to the imperial quarters.

CHAPTER VI

THEN, for a short time, the emperor did everything as the advisers appointed by his father suggested. They were with him every day, giving him wise counsel; they allowed him only as much leisure as they thought necessary for the sensible care of his body. But some of his court companions interfered and tried to corrupt the character of the naïve emperor. All the sycophants at his table, men who gauge their pleasure by their bellies and something a little lower, kept reminding him of the gay life at Rome, describing the delightful spectacles and musical shows and cataloguing the abundance of luxuries available there. They complained about wasting their time on the banks of the Danube, pointing out that the region was not productive in summer and that the fog and cold were unending. "Master," they said again and again, "when will you stop drinking this icy liquid mud? In the meantime, others will be enjoying warm streams and cool streams, mists and fine air too, all of which only Italy possesses in abundance." By merely suggesting such delights to the youth, they whetted his appetite for a taste of pleasures. And so he immediately summoned his advisers and informed them that he longed to see his native land. But, ashamed to admit the real reason for his sudden interest in returning, he pretended to be fearful that one of the wealthy aristocrats in Rome would seize the empire and, after raising an army and a rampart, take control of the empire, as if from an impregnable fortress. For the Roman populace was sufficiently large to supply numerous picked young men for such an army.

While the youth was alleging such specious excuses, the rest, sick at heart, kept their eyes fixed on the ground in dismay. But Pompeianus, the oldest of his advisers and a relation of the emperor by marriage (his wife was Commodus' oldest sister), said to him: "Child and master too, it is entirely reasonable for you to long to see your native land; we too are gripped by hunger to see those we left at home. But more important and more urgent matters here put a curb on that yearning. For the rest of your life you will have the enjoyment of things at home; and for that matter, where the emperor is, Rome is. But to leave this war unfinished is both disgraceful and dangerous. That course would increase the barbarians' boldness; they will not believe that we long to return to our home, but will rather accuse us of a cowardly retreat. After you have conquered all these barbarians and extended the boundaries of the empire to the northern seas, it will be glorious for you to return home to celebrate your triumph, leading as fettered captives barbarian kings and governors. The Romans who preceded you became famous and gained renown in this way. There is no reason to fear that

BOOK ONE

someone at home may seize control. The most distinguished senators are right here with you; the imperial troops are here to protect you; all the funds from the imperial depositories are here; and finally, the memory of your father has won for you the eternal loyalty and good will of your subjects."

7 Eager to improve the situation, Pompeianus, by his exhortations, restrained the youth for a short time. Commodus, shamed by his words and unable to make a suitable reply, dismissed the group, saying that he would consider person-
8 ally and at greater length what he should do. Then, yielding to his companions, he no longer consulted his advisers about anything. He sent off letters and, after assigning command of the Danube to men whom he considered capable, ordering them to block the barbarians' attacks, he announced his departure for Rome. Those left behind carried out their assignments; soon they subdued most of the barbarians by force of arms, and easily won the friendship of the rest by
9 substantial bribes. The barbarians are by nature fond of money; contemptuous of danger, they obtain the necessities of life either by pillaging and plundering or by selling peace at a huge price. Commodus was aware of this practice; since he had plenty of money, he bargained for release from care and gave them everything they demanded.

CHAPTER VII

WHEN the emperor's decision was announced, the army was in turmoil; all the soldiers wanted to leave with him, so that they might stop wasting their time in the war and enjoy the pleasures at Rome. When the news was circulated and messengers arrived to report the approach of the emperor, the Roman people were overjoyed; they had the highest hopes for the reign of the young emperor, believ-

MARCUS AURELIUS AND COMMODUS

ing that he would rule as his father had ruled. Speeding with the vigor of youth, Commodus passed quickly through the cities between Pannonia and Rome. Received everywhere with imperial pomp, he appeared in person before the celebrating crowds, a pleasing sight to all. As he drew near Rome, the entire senate and the people of the city cast aside all restraint. Bearing laurel branches and every kind of flower then in bloom, each man carrying as much as he could manage and eager to be first, they came out some distance from the city to welcome their young and nobly born emperor. For they did indeed give him all their affection, since he was born and reared among them and was of imperial ancestry through three generations of distinguished Romans. His father's family tree included a number of distinguished senators; his mother, the empress Faustina, was the daughter of Antoninus Pius; she was the granddaughter of Hadrian on her mother's side and traced her ancestry to Trajan, her great-grandfather.

Such was Commodus' family background. At this time he was in the prime of youth, striking in appearance, with a well-developed body and a face that was handsome without being pretty. His commanding eyes flashed like lightning; his hair, naturally blond and curly, gleamed in the sunlight as if it were on fire; some thought that he sprinkled his hair with gold dust before appearing in public, while others saw in it something divine, saying that a heavenly light shone round his head. To add to his beauty, the first down was just beginning to appear on his cheeks. This was the emperor upon whom the Romans feasted their eyes and welcomed with garlands and showers of blossoms. Entering the city,[6] Commodus went immediately to the temple of Jupiter[7] and

---
[6] October, 180.
[7] The temple of Jupiter Optimus Maximus on the Capitoline Hill.

BOOK ONE

the other shrines. After expressing his gratitude to the senate and to the soldiers on duty in Rome for their loyal protection, he entered the imperial palace.

CHAPTER VIII

FOR several years the emperor deferred to the advisers appointed by his father, following their advice in everything. But when he assumed absolute control of the empire, he put in command of the Praetorian Guard an Italian, Perennis, who seemed to be a capable soldier. (Indeed, it was for this reason that Commodus made him praetorian prefect.) Perennis indulged the emperor's youthful appetites, permitting him to spend his time in drinking and debauchery, and relieved him of imperial cares and responsibilities.

2 Perennis assumed full personal charge of the empire, driven by his insatiable lust for money, his contempt for what he had, and his greedy longing for what was not yet his. To begin with, he launched an attack upon Commodus' advisers and upon all the wealthy and nobly born; by casting suspicion upon these men, Perennis aroused the fears of the emperor and provided the youth with reason and opportunity to destroy them and confiscate their property.

3 For the present, however, the memory of his father and his respect for his advisers held Commodus in check. But then a disastrous stroke of ill fortune completely altered his previously mild, moderate disposition. It happened this way. The oldest of the emperor's sisters was Lucilla. She had formerly been married to Lucius Verus Caesar,[8] whom Marcus had made his associate in governing the empire; by marrying Lucilla to Lucius, Marcus had made her marriage

---

[8] By the late second century, the title Caesar conferred by the reigning emperor carried with it a claim to the succession. I have used "Caesar" regularly in preference to a less exact "heir."

22

MARCUS AURELIUS AND COMMODUS

to his Caesar the strongest bond of mutual good will. But after Lucius died,[9] Lucilla, who retained all the privileges of her imperial position, was married by her father to Pompeianus. Commodus, too, allowed his sister to retain the imperial honors; she continued to occupy the imperial seat at the theaters, and the sacred fire was carried before her. But when Commodus married Crispina, custom demanded that the front seat at the theater be assigned to the empress. Lucilla found this difficult to endure, and felt that any honor paid to the empress was an insult to her; but since she was well aware that her husband Pompeianus was devoted to Commodus, she told him nothing about her plans to seize control of the empire. Instead, she tested the sentiments of a wealthy young nobleman, Quadratus, with whom she was rumored to be sleeping in secret. Complaining constantly about this matter of imperial precedence, she soon persuaded the young man to set in motion a plot which brought destruction upon himself and the entire senate. Quadratus, in selecting confederates among the prominent senators, prevailed upon Quintianus, a bold and reckless young senator, to conceal a dagger beneath his robe and, watching for a suitable time and place, to stab Commodus; as for the rest, he assured Quintianus that he would set matters straight by bribes. But the assassin, standing in the entrance to the amphitheater (it was dark there and he hoped to escape detection), drew his dagger and shouted at Commodus that he had been sent by the senate to kill him. Quintianus wasted time making his little speech and waving his dagger; as a result, he was seized by the emperor's bodyguards before he could strike, and died for his stupidity in revealing the plot prematurely. Thus found out beforehand, Quintianus brought about his own death, and Commodus was put on his guard by this forewarning.

---
[9] Married to Lucilla in 164, Verus died in 169.

BOOK ONE

7 This was the initial reason for the young emperor's hatred of the senate. He took Quintianus' words to heart and, ever mindful of what his attacker had said, now considered the
8 entire senate his collective enemy. This incident also gave Perennis sufficient excuse for taking action, for he was always advising the emperor to eliminate and destroy the prominent men. By confiscating their property, Perennis easily made himself the richest man of his time. After the attempt at assassination had been thoroughly investigated by the prefect, Commodus without mercy put to death his sister, all those actually involved in the plot, and any who were under the slightest suspicion as well.

CHAPTER IX

AFTER he had removed the men whom Commodus had reason to fear, those who showed him good will for his father's sake, and those who were concerned for the emperor's safety, Perennis, now a powerful figure, began to plot for the empire. Commodus was persuaded to put the prefect's sons in command of the army of Illyricum, though they were still young men; the prefect himself amassed a huge sum of money for lavish gifts in order to incite the army to revolt. His sons quietly increased their forces, so that they might seize the empire after Perennis had disposed of Commodus.

2 This plot came to light in a curious fashion. The Romans celebrate a sacred festival in honor of Jupiter Capitolinus,[10] and all the stage shows and athletic exhibitions are sent to take part in this festival in the capital. The emperor is both spectator and judge, together with the rest of the priests,
3 who are summoned in rotation for this duty. Upon his ar-

---

[10] The *ludi Capitolini*, oldest of the Roman festivals, celebrated on October 15. Plutarch *Rom.* 25.

MARCUS AURELIUS AND COMMODUS

rival for the performance of the famous actors, Commodus took his seat in the imperial chair; an orderly crowd filled the theater, quietly occupying the assigned seats. Before any action took place on the stage, however, a man dressed as a philosopher[11] (half-naked, carrying a staff in his hand and a leather bag on his shoulder) ran out and took his stand in the center of the stage. Silencing the audience with a sweep of his hand, he said: "Commodus, this is no time to celebrate festivals and devote yourself to shows and entertainments. The sword of Perennis is at your throat. Unless you guard yourself from a danger not threatening but already upon you, you shall not escape death. Perennis himself is raising money and an army to oppose you, and his sons are winning over the army of Illyricum. Unless you act first, you shall die." Whether he said this by divine inspiration, or whether, obscure and unknown before, he was making an effort to gain fame, or hoped to receive a generous reward from the emperor—whatever the reason, Commodus was thunderstruck. Everyone was suspicious of the man's words, and no one believed him. Perennis ordered the philosopher to be seized and burned for making insane and lying accusations. Such was the penalty that the beggar paid for his ill-timed outspokenness. The emperor's intimate friends, however, who had long been secretly hostile to Perennis (for the prefect was harsh and unbearable in his insolence and arrogance), believed that the time had come and began to bring charges against him. As a result, Commodus escaped the plot, and Perennis and his sons perished miserably. For not much later, some soldiers visited Perennis' son[12] in secret and carried off coins bearing the prefect's portrait. And, without the knowledge of Perennis, the praetorian

---
[11] One of the ubiquitous Cynic beggar philosophers.
[12] The confusion concerning Perennis' sons is Herodian's: he had two sons, both of whom were presumably involved in the total plot, though Herodian follows the fate of only one.

BOOK ONE

prefect, they took the coins directly to Commodus and revealed to him the secret details of the plot. They were richly
8 rewarded for their service. While Perennis was still ignorant of these developments and anticipated nothing of the sort, the emperor sent for him at night and had him beheaded. And he dispatched men to Perennis' son by the fastest route, so that they might reach him before he knew what had happened. These men were to take a route shorter than the one by which news was regularly carried; in this way they would be able to come to the youth before he was aware of events at Rome. Commodus wrote the youth a friendly letter, telling him that he was recalling him to greater expectations,
9 and ordering him to come to Rome. Perennis' son knew nothing of the reception awaiting him and was unaware of his father's fate. When the messengers informed him that his father had given these same orders orally but, satisfied with the emperor's letter, had not written a separate note, the youth was convinced, although he was concerned about leaving the plot unfinished. Nevertheless, relying on his father's power as if that power still existed, he left Illyricum.
10 On the way to Italy the youth was killed by the emperor's men. Such was the fate of Perennis and his son. Thereafter Commodus regularly appointed two praetorian prefects, believing that it was safer not to place too much authority in the hands of one man; he hoped that this division of authority would discourage any desire to seize the imperial power.

CHAPTER X

BUT before long another plot was organized against Commodus. It involved a former soldier named Maternus, who had committed many frightful crimes. He deserted from the army, persuading others to flee with him, and soon collected a huge mob of desperadoes. At first they attacked and plundered villages and farms, but when Maternus had amassed a sizable sum of money, he gathered an even larger band of cutthroats by offering the prospect of generous booty and a fair share of the loot. As a result, his men no longer appeared to be brigands but rather enemy troops. They now attacked the largest cities and released all the prisoners, no matter what the reasons for their imprisonment. By promising these men their freedom, he persuaded them to join his band in gratitude for favors received. The bandits roamed over all Gaul and Spain, attacking the largest cities; a few of these they burned, but the rest they abandoned after sacking them. When he was informed of these developments, Commodus, in a towering rage, sent threatening dispatches to the governors of the provinces involved, charging them with negligence and ordering them to raise an army to oppose the bandits. When the brigands learned that an army was being raised against them, they left the regions which they had been ravaging and slipped unnoticed, a few at a time, into Italy, by a quick but difficult route. And now Maternus was plotting for the empire, for larger stakes indeed. Since everything he had attempted had succeeded beyond his fondest hopes, he concluded that if he were to undertake something really important it was bound to succeed; having committed himself to a hazard from which it was impossible to withdraw, he would, at least, not die obscure and unknown. But when he reflected that he did not have an army sufficiently powerful to resist Commodus on equal terms and in open opposition (for it was thought that the majority of the Roman people were still well disposed toward Commodus, and he also had the support of the Praetorian Guard), Maternus hoped to balance this inequality of forces by guile and cunning. This is the way he undertook to accomplish it.

Every year, on a set day at the beginning of spring, the

BOOK ONE

Romans celebrate a festival in honor of the mother of the gods.[18] All the valuable trappings of each deity, the imperial treasures, and marvelous objects of all kinds, both natural and man-made, are carried in procession before this goddess. Free license for every kind of revelry is granted, and each man assumes the disguise of his choice. No office is so important or so sacrosanct that permission is refused anyone to put on its distinctive uniform and join in the revelry, concealing his true identity; consequently, it is not easy to distinguish the true from the false. This seemed to Maternus an ideal time to launch his plot undetected. By donning the uniform of a praetorian soldier and outfitting his companions in the same way, he hoped to mingle with the true praetorians and, after watching part of the parade, to attack Commodus and kill him while no one was on guard. But the plan was betrayed when some of those who had accompanied him into the city revealed the plot. (Jealousy led them to disclose it, since they preferred to be ruled by the emperor rather than by a bandit chief.) Before he arrived at the scene of the festivities, Maternus was seized and beheaded, and his companions suffered the punishment they deserved. After sacrificing to the goddess and making thank offerings, Commodus completed the festivities and did honor to the goddess, rejoicing at his escape. The people continued to celebrate their emperor's deliverance after the festival came to an end.

CHAPTER XI

AS WE have discovered by research, the Romans are devoted to this goddess for the following reason—a reason which it seems worth while to relate here, since it is un-

---

[18] The rites of the spring festival in honor of Cybele, goddess of fertility, began on March 15.

known to some of the Greeks. They say that this statue of the goddess fell from the sky;[14] the exact material of the statue is not known, nor the identity of the artists who made it; in fact, it is not certain that the statue was the work of human hands. Long ago it fell from the sky in Phrygia (the name of the region where it fell is Pessinus, which received its name from the fall of the heavenly statue); the statue was discovered there. As we learn from other sources, a battle is said to have taken place there between Ilus the Phrygian and Tantalus the Lydian. Some say it was a boundary dispute; others, that it was concerned with Ganymede's kidnaping.[15] The battle continued for a long time on even terms, and a large number of men fell on both sides; this disaster gave the region its name. It was there, so the story goes, that Ganymede was spirited away and disappeared from mortals' view when his brother and lover tore him limb from limb. After the youth's body vanished, his sufferings made him immortal when Zeus spirited him away to heaven. The Phrygians of old staged their revels in Pessinus, on the banks of the river Gallus, from which the eunuch priests of Cybele derive their name. When Roman affairs prospered, they say that an oracle prophesied that the empire would endure and soar to greater heights if the goddess were brought from Pessinus to Rome. The Romans therefore sent an embassy to Phrygia and asked for the statue; they easily got it by reminding the Phrygians of their kinship and by recalling to them that Aeneas the Phrygian was the ancestor of the Romans. The statue was carried aboard ship, but when the vessel arrived at the mouth of the Tiber (the Romans use this as their harbor) it came to a halt, stopped by divine power. For a long time the Romans tried in every way to dislodge

---

[14] These heaven-sent statues derive from the Palladium, a sacred image of Athena sent down by Zeus to the founders of Troy.
[15] Ovid *Met.* 10.155 ff.

BOOK ONE

the ship, which was held fast as if by a sand bar, but it refused to move until one of the Vestal Virgins, who was charged with breaking her oath of chastity, was led forward. The priestess, who was about to be put to death, begged the people to submit her case to the goddess from Pessinus. She unfastened the sash at her waist and attached it to the prow of the ship, praying that if she were still virgin and pure the ship would follow her. The ship, secured to her sash, followed her readily. The Romans were struck with awe both by the manifestation of the goddess and by the piety of the maiden.[16] Let this suffice as an inquiry into the history of the goddess from Pessinus, but it will prove a not unwelcome digression to those unfamiliar with Roman affairs. After escaping Maternus' plot, Commodus strengthened his personal bodyguard and seldom appeared in public. He spent most of his time at his suburban estate and at the imperial estates far from Rome, having given up his judicial and administrative duties.

CHAPTER XII

ABOUT this time, plague struck all Italy. The suffering was especially severe in Rome, since the city, which received people from all over the world, was overcrowded. The city suffered great loss of both men and animals. Then, on the advice of his physicians, Commodus left Rome for Laurentum.[17] This region enjoyed the shade from extensive laurel groves (whence the area derives its name); it was cooler there and seemed to be a safe haven. The emperor is said to have counteracted the pollution in the air by the fragrant scent of the laurels and the refreshing shade of the trees. At the direction of their doctors, those who remained in Rome

---

[16] Cf. Livy 29.10; Ovid *Fasti* 4.305 ff.; Seneca *Frag.* 80; Suetonius *Tib.* 2.
[17] A few miles south of Rome on the seacoast.

filled their nostrils and ears with fragrant oils and used perfume and incense constantly, for some said that the sweet odor, entering first, filled up the sensory passages and kept out the poison in the air; or, if any poison should enter, it would be neutralized by the stronger odors. The plague, however, continued to rage unchecked for a long time, and many men died, as well as domestic animals of all kinds.

Famine gripped the city at the same time. Responsible for it was a Phrygian named Cleander, one of the slaves offered for sale by the public auctioneer for the benefit of the state. As a slave in the imperial household, Cleander grew up with Commodus and eventually was raised to a position of honor and authority: the command of the bodyguard, the stewardship of the imperial bedroom, and the control of the imperial armies were all entrusted to him. Because of his wealth and wantonness, Cleander coveted the empire. He bought up most of the grain supply and put it in storage; he hoped in this way to get control of the people and the army by making a generous distribution of grain at the first sign of a food shortage, anticipating that he would win the support of the people when they were suffering from a scarcity of food. He also built a huge gymnasium and public bath and turned them over to the people. In this way he tried to curry favor with the mob. The Romans, however, hated the man and blamed him for all their difficulties; they especially despised him for his greed. At first they attacked him bitterly when they thronged the theaters; later, however, they went in a body to Commodus, who was passing the time on his estate near the city, and there, raising a fearful din, they demanded Cleander for execution. During this tumult on the grounds of his suburban estate, Commodus was loitering in the pleasant, secluded inner rooms, for Cleander had kept him in ignorance of what was happening. Suddenly, unlooked for by the assembled mob, the imperial cavalry appeared fully

BOOK ONE

7 armed and, at the order of the prefect, butchered those in their path. The people were unable to withstand the assault, for they were unarmed men on foot fighting against armed men on horseback. And so they fell, not only because they were attacked by the cavalry and trampled by the horses, but also because they were overwhelmed by the sheer weight
8 of their own numbers, and many died in the pile-ups. The horsemen pursued the fugitives right to the gates of Rome and slaughtered them without mercy as they attempted to force their way into the city. When those who had remained in Rome heard what had happened, they blocked the doors of their houses and went up on the roofs to throw down stones and roof tiles on the cavalry, who now suffered what they had inflicted, for no one opposed them in formal battle; most of the people were hurling missiles at them from safe positions. Finally, unable to endure the onslaught any longer, the wounded horsemen turned and fled, leaving many dead
9 behind. In the steady hail of missiles, their horses stumbled and fell on the round stones, throwing their riders. After many had been killed on both sides, the infantry in the city, who despised the cavalry, came to the aid of the mob.

CHAPTER XIII

EVEN though a civil war was raging, no one was willing to report to Commodus what was happening, for fear of Cleander. Finally the emperor's eldest sister (her name was Phadilla) rushed into the palace (as his sister, she had free and easy access to the emperor), and, loosing her hair, threw
2 herself down and cried out in anguish: "Here you are, emperor, taking your leisure, ignorant of what is happening, when you are actually in the gravest danger. And we, your own flesh and blood, are at this very moment threatened with murder. Already the Roman people and most of the army

MARCUS AURELIUS AND COMMODUS

are lost to you. What we would not think of enduring at the hands of barbarians, our own people are doing to us. And those people whom you have treated with special consideration, you now find to be your enemies. Cleander has armed the people and the soldiers against you. Those who hate him because they hold differing opinions, the mob, and the entire imperial cavalry, who support him, are up in arms, killing each other and choking the city with blood. The fury of both factions will fall upon us unless you immediately hand over to them for execution this scoundrelly servant of yours, who already has been the cause of so much destruction for the people and who threatens to be the cause of so much destruction for us." After she had made these statements, tearing her clothes in grief, others who were present (for they became bolder at the words of the emperor's sister) urged Commodus to take action. He was terrified by this pressing danger, which did not merely threaten but was already upon him. In his panic he sent for Cleander, who knew nothing of what had been reported to the emperor, but had his suspicions. When the prefect appeared, Commodus ordered him seized and beheaded, and, impaling his head on a long spear, sent it out to the mob, to whom it was a welcome and long-desired sight. In this way he terminated the danger, and both sides stopped fighting: the soldiers, because they saw that the man for whom they had been fighting had been killed and also because they feared the wrath of the emperor (for they realized that he had been deceived and that Cleander had done everything without imperial approval); the people, because their desire for vengeance was satisfied by the arrest of the man responsible for the appalling crimes. They put Cleander's children to death (for he had two sons), and killed all his known friends. They dragged their bodies through the streets, subjecting them to every indignity, and finally brought the mutilated corpses to the sewer and threw them

BOOK ONE

in. Such was the fate of Cleander and his associates; it was as if Nature had undertaken to demonstrate that a small and unexpected twist of fate can raise a man from the lowest depths to the greatest heights and then plunge the man so exalted down to the depths again.

7 Although he feared a popular uprising and a new attempt upon his life, Commodus nevertheless, at the urging of his advisers, entered the city. Received there with great enthusiasm, he went to the imperial palace, escorted by the people. After undergoing such risks, the emperor trusted no one; he killed now without warning, listening to all accusations without question and paying no heed to those worthy of a hearing. He no longer had any regard for the "good life"; night and day, without interruption, licentious pleasures of
8 the flesh made him a slave, body and soul. Men of intelligence and those who had even a smattering of learning were driven from the palace as conspirators, but the emperor gave enthralled attention to the filthy skits of comedians and actors. He took lessons in driving the chariot and trained to take part in the wild-animal fights; his flatterers praised these activities as proof of his manliness, but he indulged in them more often than befitted an intelligent emperor.

CHAPTER XIV

IN THAT time of crisis a number of divine portents occurred. Stars remained visible during the day; other stars, extending to an enormous length, seemed to be hanging in the middle of the sky. Abnormal animals were born, strange
2 in shape and deformed of limb. But the worst portent of all, which aggravated the present crisis and disturbed those who employ auguries and omens to predict the future, was this. Although no massing of dark clouds and no thunderstorm preceded it, and only a slight earthquake occurred before-

hand, either as a result of a lightning bolt at night or a fire which broke out after the earthquake, the temple of Peace,[18] the largest and most beautiful building in the city, was totally destroyed by fire. It was the richest of all the temples, and, because it was a safe place, was adorned with offerings of gold and silver; every man deposited his possessions there. But this fire, in a single night, made paupers of many rich men. All Rome joined in mourning the public loss, and each man lamented his own personal loss.

After consuming the temple and the entire sacred precinct, the fire swept on to destroy a large part of the city, including its most beautiful buildings. When the temple of Vesta went up in flames, the image of Pallas Athena was exposed to public view—that statue which the Romans worship and keep hidden, the one brought from Troy, as the story goes.[19] Now, for the first time since its journey from Troy to Italy, the statue was seen by men of our time. For the Vestal Virgins snatched up the image and carried it along the Sacred Way to the imperial palace. Many other beautiful sections of the city were destroyed in this fire, which continued to burn for days, spreading in all directions. It was not finally extinguished until falling showers put an end to its raging. For this reason the disaster was held to be of divine origin; in that critical period, men believed that the fire was started and stopped by the will and power of the gods. Some conjectured from these events that the destruction of the temple of Peace was a prophecy of war. And subsequent events, as we shall relate in the books to follow, confirmed this prophecy by actual events.

---

[18] This temple, in the Forum of Peace, was begun by Vespasian in 71 to commemorate the capture of Jerusalem.

[19] According to legend, the true Palladium was sent down from heaven by Zeus to Dardanus, founder of Troy, or to his descendant Ilus. Brought to Italy by Aeneas, also according to legend, it was placed in the temple of Vesta to protect the city of Rome.

BOOK ONE

7 With so many disasters befalling the city in rapid succession, the Roman people no longer looked with favor upon Commodus; they attributed their misfortunes to his illegal murders and the other mistakes he had made in his lifetime. He no longer concealed his activities, nor did he have any desire to keep them secret. What they objected to his doing in private he now had the effrontery to do in public. He fell
8 into a state of drunken madness. First he discarded his family name and issued orders that he was to be called not Commodus, son of Marcus, but Hercules, son of Zeus. Abandoning the Roman and imperial mode of dress, he donned the lion skin, and carried the club of Hercules. He wore purple robes embroidered with gold, making himself an object of ridicule by combining in one set of garments the frailty of
9 a woman and the might of a superman. This was the way he looked in his public appearances. He assigned new names to the months of the year; abolishing the old ones, he called the months after his own list of names and titles, most of which actually referred to Hercules as the manliest of men.[20] He erected statues of himself throughout the city, but opposite the senate house he set up a special statue representing the emperor as an archer poised to shoot, for he wished even his statues to inspire fear of him.

CHAPTER XV

THE senate removed this statue of Commodus after his death and replaced it with a statue of Freedom. Now the emperor, casting aside all restraint, took part in the public shows, promising to kill with his own hands wild animals of all kinds and to fight in gladiatorial combat against the bravest of the youths. When this news became known, people hastened to Rome from all over Italy and from the neigh-

---

[20] Cf. Dio 73.15.3. Also A. Lampridius *Vita Commod.* 11.8.

MARCUS AURELIUS AND COMMODUS

boring provinces to see what they had neither seen nor even heard of before. Special mention was made of the skill of his hands and the fact that he never missed when hurling javelins or shooting arrows. His instructors were the most skillful of the Parthian bowmen and the most accurate of the Moroccan javelin men, but he surpassed them all in marksmanship. When the days for the show arrived, the amphitheater was completely filled. A terrace encircling the arena had been constructed for Commodus, enabling him to avoid risking his life by fighting the animals at close quarters; rather, by hurling his javelins down from a safe place, he offered a display of skill rather than of courage. Deer, roebuck, and horned animals of all kinds, except bulls, he struck down, running with them in pursuit, anticipating their dashes, and killing them with deadly blows. Lions, leopards, and other animals of the nobler sort he killed from above, running around on his terrace. And on no occasion did anyone see a second javelin used, nor any wound except the death wound. For at the very moment the animal started up, it received the blow on its forehead or in its heart, and it bore no other wound, nor did the javelin pierce any other part of its body: the beast was wounded and killed in the same instant. Animals were collected for him from all over the world. Then we saw in the flesh animals that we had previously marveled at in paintings. From India and Ethiopia, from lands to the north and to the south, any animals hitherto unknown he displayed to the Romans and then dispatched them. On one occasion he shot arrows with crescent-shaped heads at Moroccan ostriches, birds that move with great speed, both because of their swiftness afoot and the sail-like nature of their wings. He cut off their heads at the very top of the neck; so, after their heads had been severed by the edge of the arrow, they continued to run around as if they had not been injured. Once when a leopard, with a lightning dash, seized a condemned criminal, he thwarted the leopard with his javelin as it was about to close its jaws; he killed the beast and rescued the man, the point of the javelin anticipating the points of the leopard's teeth. Again, when a hundred lions appeared in one group as if from beneath the earth, he killed the entire hundred with exactly one hundred javelins, and all the bodies lay stretched out in a straight line for some distance; they could thus be counted with no difficulty, and no one saw a single extra javelin.

7 As far as these activities are concerned, however, even if his conduct was hardly becoming for an emperor, he did win the approval of the mob for his courage and his marksmanship. But when he came into the amphitheater naked, took up arms, and fought as a gladiator, the people saw a disgraceful spectacle, a nobly born emperor of the Romans, whose fathers and forebears had won many victories, not taking the field against barbarians or opponents worthy of the Romans, but disgracing his high position by degrading 8 and disgusting exhibitions. In his gladiatorial combats, he defeated his opponents with ease, and he did no more than wound them, since they all submitted to him, but only because they knew he was the emperor, not because he was truly a gladiator. At last he became so demented that he was unwilling to live in the imperial palace, but wished to change his residence to the gladiatorial barracks. He gave orders that he was no longer to be called Hercules, but by the name 9 of a famous gladiator then dead. He removed the head of a huge Colossus[21] which the Romans worship and which bears the likeness of the Sun, replacing it with his own head, and inscribed on the base not the usual imperial and family titles; instead of "Germanicus" he wrote: "Conqueror of a Thousand Gladiators."

---

[21] Originally a colossal statue of Nero, for whose head Vespasian substituted a head of the Sun. Suetonius *Vesp.* 18.

CHAPTER XVI

BUT the time had finally come for Commodus to cease his mad antics and for the Roman empire to be rid of this tyrant. This occurred on the first day of the new year,[22] when the Romans celebrate the festival which they trace back to the most ancient of the Italic native gods. They believe that Saturn, ousted from his realm by Jupiter, came down to earth and was the guest of Janus. Fearful of his son's power, he escaped when Janus hid him. This episode gave the region of Latium its name, which is derived from the Greek word *lathein,* "to escape notice." For this reason the Italians continue to celebrate the Saturnalia down to the present time, to commemorate the sheltering of the god, and they observe at the beginning of the year the festival of the Italic god Janus. The statues of Janus have two faces because the year begins and ends with him. On the day of this festival the Romans go out of their way to greet each other and exchange gifts. On this day, too, they dine together gaily on the delicacies of land and sea. This is also the day on which the consuls who give their names to the year first don the purple robes of office for their one-year term. When all were occupied in the celebration, Commodus had it in mind to appear not from the imperial palace, in the customary fashion, but from the gladiatorial barracks, clad in armor instead of in the splendid imperial purple, and accompanied by the rest of the gladiators.

He announced his intentions to Marcia, whom, of all his mistresses, he held in highest esteem; he kept nothing from this woman, as if she were his legal wife, even allowing her the imperial honors except for the sacred fire. When she learned of his plan, so unreasonable and unbecoming an

---
[22] Actually the night of December 31, 192.

BOOK ONE

emperor, she threw herself at his feet, entreating him, with tears, not to bring disgrace upon the Roman empire and not to endanger his life by entrusting it to gladiators and desperate men. After much pleading, unable to persuade the emperor to abandon his plan, she left him, still weeping. Commodus then summoned Laetus, the praetorian prefect, and Eclectus, his bedroom steward, and ordered them to make arrangements for him to spend the night in the gladiatorial barracks, telling them that he would leave for the festival sacrifices from there, and show himself to the Romans under arms. And these men, too, pleaded with the emperor not to do anything unworthy of his imperial position.

CHAPTER XVII

COMMODUS, enraged, dismissed them and retired to his bedroom for a nap (for this was his custom in the middle of the day). First he took a wax tablet—one made from a thin strip of basswood, which grows under the bark of the linden tree—and wrote down the names of those who 2 were to be put to death that night. Marcia's name was at the top of the list, followed by Laetus and Eclectus and a large number of the foremost senators. Commodus wanted all the elder statesmen and the advisers appointed for him by his father, those who still survived, to be put to death, for he was ashamed to have these revered men witness his disgraceful actions. He planned to confiscate the property of the wealthy and distribute it to the soldiers, so that they would protect him, and to the gladiators, so that they would entertain him. 3 After composing his list, Commodus placed the tablet on his couch, thinking that no one would come into his bedroom. But there was in the palace a very young little boy, one of those who went about bare of clothes but adorned with gold and costly gems. The Roman voluptuaries always took delight in these lads. Commodus was very fond of this child and often slept with him; his name, Philocommodus, clearly indicates the emperor's affection for him. Philocommodus was playing idly about the palace. After Commodus had gone out to his usual baths and drinking bouts, the lad wandered into the emperor's bedroom, as he usually did; picking up the tablet for a plaything, he left the bedroom. By a stroke of fate, he met Marcia. After hugging and kissing him (for she too was fond of the child), she took the tablet from him, afraid that in his heedless play he might accidentally erase something important. When she recognized the emperor's handwriting, she was eager to read the tablet. Discovering that it was a death list and that she was scheduled to die first, followed by Laetus and Eclectus and many others marked for murder, she cried out in grief and then said to herself: "So, Commodus, this is my reward for my love and devotion, after I have put up with your arrogance and your madness for so many years. But, you drunken sot, you shall not outwit a woman deadly sober!" She then summoned Eclectus; he was in the habit of visiting her anyway, since he was the bedroom steward, and it was rumored that she was sleeping with him. She handed him the tablet, saying: "See what a party we are to enjoy tonight!" Eclectus read it and was dumfounded (but he was an Egyptian, bold by nature and quick-tempered, a man of action). Sealing the tablet, he sent it off to Laetus by one of his trusted slaves. After reading the tablet, Laetus hurried to Marcia as if to discuss the emperor's orders with her, especially about his proposed stay with the gladiators. And while they pretended to be arguing about this matter, they concluded that they must act first or suffer the consequences, agreeing that it was no time for indecision or delay. They decided to poison Commodus, and Marcia assured them that she could administer a potion with the greatest ease. For it was her custom to mix the wine and give the

BOOK ONE

emperor his first cup, so that he might have a pleasant drink from the hand of his beloved. When Commodus returned from his bath, she poured the poison into the cup, mixed it with a pungent wine, and gave it to him to drink. Since it was his practice to take a cup of friendship after his many baths and jousts with animals, he drained it without noticing anything unusual. Immediately he became drowsy and stupefied and fell asleep, believing that it was the natural result of his exertions. Eclectus and Marcia ordered all the rest to return to their homes, and made everything quiet for him. Commodus had acted like this on other occasions when overcome by wine. Since he bathed often and drank often, he had no set time for sleeping; in addition, he indulged in all kinds of pleasures, to which he was a willing slave at any hour. For a short time he lay quiet, but, when the poison spread through his stomach and bowels, he became nauseated and began to vomit violently, either because his excessive eating and drinking were expelling the poison, or because he had taken beforehand an antidote for poison, as emperors regularly did before eating or drinking. After much vomiting had occurred, the conspirators, afraid that Commodus would get rid of the poison, recover, and kill them, promised lavish rewards to a powerful young nobleman, Narcissus, if he would strangle the emperor. Narcissus rushed in where the emperor lay overcome by the poisoned wine, seized him by the throat, and finished him off.

Such was the fate Commodus suffered, after ruling for thirteen years from the date of his father's death. He was the most nobly born of all the emperors who preceded him and was the handsomest man of his time, both in beauty of features and in physical development. If it were fitting to discuss his manly qualities, he was inferior to no man in skill and in marksmanship, if only he had not disgraced these excellent traits by shameful practices.

BOOK TWO

PERTINAX, DIDIUS JULIANUS

CHAPTER I

AFTER the conspirators had killed Commodus, as has been described in the first book of our history, they were anxious to keep the deed secret. And so, to prevent the praetorians on guard in the imperial palace from discovering what they had done, they wrapped the emperor's body in bed linen and tied it securely. They gave the bundle to two loyal slaves and sent it out of the palace as if it were no more than laundry, somewhat bulkier than usual. The slaves carried their burden past the guards; some of them were asleep, overcome by wine, others still awake, but dozing off leaning on their spears. The praetorians made no attempt to discover the contents of the bundle carried from the emperor's bedroom, since it was not their concern to look into such things. After the emperor's body had been carried out through the palace gates undetected, it was placed in a wagon and taken to the outskirts of the city.

Then Laetus and Eclectus conferred with Marcia about

BOOK TWO

the best course to follow. They decided that an announcement should be made to the effect that the emperor had died suddenly of apoplexy. They were sure that this report would be accepted without question by those who heard it, since his endless and excessive orgies had prepared them for such an outcome. But before doing anything else, the conspirators thought it best to choose a sensible elder statesman as the successor to the throne, both to save themselves and to bring to all enjoyment of a respite from a tyrant so harsh and undisciplined. Discussing the matter among themselves, they found no man so well qualified for the post as a native-born

4 Italian named Pertinax. This Pertinax was famous for his accomplishments, both civil and military; he had won many victories over the Germans and the Eastern barbarians and was the only survivor of the revered advisers appointed for Commodus by his father. Commodus had not had him put to death—this most distinguished of Marcus' companions and generals—either out of respect for his noble qualities or indifference to him as a pauper. And yet his poverty had contributed in no small measure to the universal praise Pertinax enjoyed; for, despite responsibilities which far outweighed those of his colleagues, he was less wealthy than any of them.

5 That night, while all were sleeping, Laetus and Eclectus, accompanied by a few fellow conspirators, came to Pertinax. Standing at the locked gates of his house, they aroused the porter on guard there. When the man awoke and saw the soldiers standing before the gates with Laetus, whom he knew to be the praetorian prefect, he was alarmed and went

6 inside to report to his master. Pertinax directed his visitors to enter, remarking that the fate he had been expecting was at last about to overtake him. Yet even in this extremity, they say, he remained so serene that he did not get up, but received them lying in bed. Even though he believed that Laetus had come with Eclectus to kill him, he spoke to them calmly,

PERTINAX, DIDIUS JULIANUS

with no sign of pallor. "For a long time now," he said, "I have been waiting for my life to end in this fashion, and I was surprised that Commodus was so slow to act against me, the sole survivor of the advisers his father appointed for him. Why do you delay? You will be carrying out your orders, and I will be relieved from degrading hope and constant fear." To this Laetus replied: "Please stop saying things unworthy of you and your past conduct. Our visit does not concern your death but our safety and the safety of the Roman empire. The tyrant is dead, victim of a fate he richly deserved. What he planned to do to us, we have done to him. We have come to place the empire in your hands, aware that you are not only the most distinguished senator, because of your moderate life, and have won reverence for your greatness and the dignity of your years, but you also enjoy the love and esteem of the people. All these reasons lead us to believe that what we are doing will please the people and save our own lives." Pertinax said in reply: "Why do you mock an old man? Why do you judge me such a coward that you wish first to taunt and then to kill me?" At this point Eclectus spoke up: "If you do not believe what we say, read this tablet (you know Commodus' handwriting—you see it regularly). From this you will see the danger we have escaped, and you will know that there is no treachery but only truth in what we tell you." After he had read the tablet, Pertinax believed these old friends of his. Now fully understanding everything that had occurred, he placed himself at their disposal.

CHAPTER II

THEY decided that as the first step Pertinax should go to the praetorian camp to learn the attitude of the soldiers of the guard. Laetus undertook to secure the support of the

BOOK TWO

praetorians, since they owed him, as their commanding officer, a measure of respect. Accompanied by all those present, they set out for the praetorian camp. The night had almost passed, and the festival was about to begin; so everything had to be done before daybreak. A number of trusted men were sent out to spread the news that Commodus was dead and that Pertinax was on his way to the praetorian camp to take command of the empire. When these events became known, the people milled about in a frenzy of joy, like men possessed, and everyone took delight in telling the news to his neighbors, especially if they happened to be men of wealth and position, for Commodus was particularly dangerous to such men. Rushing to the temples and altars, the people united in giving thanks to the gods, shouting all sorts of things: "The tyrant is dead!" "The gladiator is slain!" and other blasphemies more scurrilous. All the insults which had hitherto been left unsaid through fear were now voiced openly, with freedom and safety restored. Most of the people ran swiftly to the praetorian camp, because they feared that the praetorians would be reluctant to accept Pertinax as emperor. Indeed, they suspected that in the future these soldiers would show little moderation; they were conditioned to blind obedience to a tyrant and were masters in the use of violence. All the people therefore went out to the camp to force the praetorians to submit. They were in the camp when Laetus and Eclectus arrived, bringing Pertinax with them. Laetus then ordered the praetorians to assemble and addressed them as follows:

"Commodus, your emperor, is dead of apoplexy. In a case of this kind, the blame can be put on no one else. The emperor was responsible for his own death. He paid no attention when we urged him time and again to adopt a safer and saner course. You know the way he lived his life. Now he lies dead, choked by his own gluttony. The death he was destined for has overtaken him at last. As you are aware, the cause of death is not one and the same for all men. The most diverse causes bring us to life's inevitable outcome. In place of Commodus we bring to you, and the whole Roman people bring to you, a man respected for his years, temperate in his way of life, and renowned for his courageous exploits. You old soldiers have taken part in his military campaigns, and the rest of you always held him in high honor and esteem during his years of service as prefect of the city. Now Fortune is giving you an emperor who is also a kindly father to you. His reign will please not only you praetorian soldiers on duty here in Rome but also the soldiers stationed on the banks of the far-off rivers and the borders of the Roman empire, men who are familiar with his exploits from their own recollections of them. No longer will we pacify the barbarians with money. They will obey us because they fear us, mindful of what they suffered at this man's hands when he campaigned against them."

After this speech of Laetus, the people restrained themselves no longer. While the praetorians were still hesitating, undecided, the people proclaimed Pertinax emperor, calling him father and shouting his praises to all. At this the soldiers, not because they were equally enthusiastic but because they were compelled by the great number of people present (they were surrounded by the mob and were themselves few in number and unarmed, as was customary during the festival), at last added their voices to the others and proclaimed Pertinax emperor. After they had sworn the usual oaths in his name and had performed the sacrifices, all the people, together with the praetorians, took up laurel branches and escorted Pertinax to the imperial palace just before daylight.

CHAPTER III

AFTER he was established in the imperial palace, to which he had been escorted by the praetorians and the people by night, as has been related above, Pertinax was beset by serious doubts; indeed, although in all matters he gave the appearance of being calm and courageous, in the present situation he was very apprehensive. The emperor was little concerned about his own safety (he had many times scorned much greater dangers), but he was worried about this abrupt change from the autocracy of Commodus and about the noble ancestry of certain of the senators. He suspected that these senators, after having been ruled by the most nobly born of all the emperors, would not be willing to let the reins of government fall into the hands of a man who came to the high

2 office from humble and undistinguished antecedents. Even if his life deserved admiration for its restraint, and even if his military exploits were famous, in nobility of birth he was much inferior to the aristocracy. When daylight came, he went to the senate house, but he did not allow the sacred fire to be carried before him nor did he permit any of the imperial tokens to be raised until he had determined how the senate

3 felt about the situation. But as soon as he appeared, all the senators with one voice shouted his praises, calling him emperor and Augustus. At first he declined the envy-provoking title of emperor and, pleading his advanced years, begged to be permitted to decline the honor, pointing out that there were many men of noble birth by whom the empire might more fittingly be ruled. At this, Glabrionus took him by the hand and led him forward, bidding him take his seat upon

4 the imperial throne. This Glabrionus was the most nobly born of all the Roman aristocrats (for he traced his ancestry to Aeneas, son of Venus and Anchises, and he had served two

PERTINAX, DIDIUS JULIANUS

terms as consul. "I myself," Glabrionus said, "whom you consider the most eligible of all, yield the throne to you, and I together with all the rest happily concur in awarding you the supreme power." Then, with all of them pleading with him and actually forcing him to accept the position, Pertinax mounted the imperial throne slowly and reluctantly and addressed the senate as follows:

"I am persuaded that your great readiness to do me honor, the extraordinary enthusiasm with which you acclaim me, and your selection of me as emperor in preference to those among you of such noble birth, has in it not the slightest intent to flatter, but is proof and pledge of your good will toward me. And this might make another ready and eager to accept without hesitation what has been entrusted to him, and he might reasonably entertain a hope of managing the empire with no difficulty among subjects so kindly disposed toward him. But these favors which I am receiving at your hands, so great and so flattering, although I am aware of the honor they do me, cause me no little apprehension and inner conflict. For, when the initial favors are so great, it is always difficult to do equal favors in return. Now when anyone who receives small favors does greater favors in return, the fact that this is an easy matter is never taken into consideration; it is thought to be merely evidence of his gratitude. But when the initial favor is virtually unsurpassable, if the recipient does not return one equally large, the fact that this is a difficult matter is never taken into consideration; it is thought to be merely evidence of his ingratitude and lack of appreciation. I see, therefore, that no ordinary task awaits me in proving myself worthy of such an honor as you have bestowed upon me. But the honor of the throne lies not in the throne itself, but in the acts which he who holds it must perform if he is not to disgrace his high office. The more men hate an unpleasant past, the more hopefully they look forward to a

BOOK TWO

pleasant future. Injuries are remembered forever (the memory of pain is difficult to erase), but benefits and the memory of benefits disappear when the enjoyment of them is gone.
8 Freedom is never so pleasant as slavery is unpleasant, and no one ever considers himself fortunate to possess what is his free from danger; he thinks that he is simply enjoying his own possessions. But the man who is deprived of his property never forgets the man responsible for his loss. And if any change takes place for the common good, no one thinks that he has derived from it any personal benefit, since, when the common good prospers, it is of little concern to the whole group as individuals. With respect to his own affairs, no one believes that anything is of value to him unless he happens
9 to obtain something he personally desires. But those who have grown accustomed to reveling in the extravagant excesses of a tyranny not only object to any change toward a more moderate and more economical way of life occasioned by a shortage of money, not terming it sensible economy or planned and judicious management, but they reject it as a mean and wretched way to live, oblivious to the fact that had it not been for the loot taken by pillage and plunder, they could never have enjoyed their luxurious way of life. On the other hand, to give to every man all things according to his worth and for logical reasons, without committing any injustices, and not to supply him with an abundance of money gained from illegal sources teaches prudent conservation of
10 things supplied in quantity. And so you, who are skilled in these matters, must coöperate with me and consider the management of the empire as a joint enterprise, and you must entertain high hopes of living under an aristocracy, not under a tyranny, and you must confirm this for all our subjects."
11 By this speech, Pertinax encouraged the senators and received the plaudits of them all. After awarding him every

PERTINAX, DIDIUS JULIANUS

honor and every token of respect, they escorted the new emperor to the temple of Jupiter and the rest of the shrines; when he had completed the sacrifices for his reign, he entered the imperial palace.

CHAPTER IV

WHEN Pertinax' speech to the senate and his letters to the people were made public, all the Romans gave thanks, hoping that he would be for them not so much an emperor as a mild and pious ruler and father. He ordered the praetorians to curb their arrogant treatment of the people; he forbade them to carry axes or strike anyone they chanced to meet. He tried to manage everything with decency and discipline, and in his judicial duties he was mild and moderate. By his consistent and deliberate imitation of Marcus' reign, he delighted the older people, and won the good will of the others without difficulty, released as they were from savage and oppressive tyranny to lead a well-ordered life, free from care. When the mildness of his rule became known everywhere, all nations subject to Roman rule or friendly to the Romans, and all the armies in the field as well, came to regard his reign as that of a god. And indeed, the barbarians who were formerly restless and rebellious, mindful of his brilliant achievements in his previous campaigns, feared him and willingly submitted to him. They put their trust in his reputation for never purposely doing an injustice and always treating every man according to his deserts; improper conduct and savage violence were completely foreign to his nature. Embassies from all countries came to him, and everyone delighted in the rule of the Romans under Pertinax.

All, both publicly and privately, were pleased by the order and the moderation of his reign. But what pleased all the

BOOK TWO

rest only galled the soldiers of the imperial bodyguard stationed in Rome. Now forbidden to loot and act with insolence, the praetorians were directed to return to an orderly and disciplined way of life. Since they considered the mild and moderate rule of Pertinax an insult and disgrace to them, as well as a diminution of their unlimited power, they refused
5 to tolerate his well-ordered reign any longer. At the beginning, they had obeyed his orders reluctantly and mutinously. But after he had been emperor for less than two months, during which he had put into effect in a short time many moderate and practical measures, and his subjects were just beginning to entertain high hopes for the future, a wretched turn of fortune upset the situation and ruined everything, preventing a number of excellent projects useful to his subjects from being carried to completion.
6 To begin with, Pertinax assigned all the land in Italy and the rest of the provinces not under cultivation to anyone willing to care for it and farm it, to be his own private property; he gave to each man as much land as he wished and was able to manage, even if the land were imperial property. To these farmers he granted exemption from all taxes for ten
7 years and freedom from government duties as well.[1] He refused to allow his name to be stamped on imperial property, stating that these effects were not the emperor's personal property but the common and public possessions of the Roman empire. Finally, he removed the tolls previously levied during the tyranny as an easy method of raising revenue, the fees collected at the banks of rivers, the harbors of cities, and the crossroads, restoring to all these their ancient freedom.
8 It is obvious that he would have done even more to benefit his subjects, as his general policy makes plain, for he banished informers from the city and ordered them to be persecuted

---

[1] The plague and the frontier wars during Marcus Aurelius' reign had seriously reduced the number of farmers in the empire.

PERTINAX, DIDIUS JULIANUS

elsewhere; he took precautions to prevent anyone from being threatened by informers or being embroiled in their false charges. Then the senate particularly, but all other men too, seemed to be living in a blessed state of security. Pertinax was so modest and unassuming that he did not bring his own son, then a young man, into the imperial palace. The youth remained in his father's house and continued to attend his regular school and gymnasium; in his education, as in all his activities, he was an ordinary Roman citizen, and displayed none of the imperial pomp and arrogance.

CHAPTER V

IN A WAY of life so prosperous and well ordered, only the praetorians complained of their lot. Longing for a return to the violence and looting of the preceding tyranny and to their extravagant and dissolute pursuits, they plotted to remove Pertinax on the ground that he was a burden and a nuisance to them, and to choose an emperor who would restore to them their unbridled and uncontrolled power. And so, with no warning, the praetorians rushed headlong from their camp one day at noon, when they were off duty. Wild with unreasoning anger, they burst into the palace with spears raised and swords drawn. The imperial attendants on duty in the palace were astounded at this unbelievable and unexpected assault. Since they were only a handful of unarmed men against a horde of armed soldiers, the attendants deserted their assigned posts and fled into the palace grounds or the nearby passageways. But a few who were devoted to Pertinax informed him of the attack and advised him to flee and put his hope of safety in the people. The emperor, however, did not follow the advice of those who suggested this advantageous course of action in the present emergency; he considered this solution undignified and servile, unworthy

BOOK TWO

of an emperor and unworthy of his previous way of life and his achievements. He therefore declined to flee or to hide; preferring to face the issue squarely, he came out to talk to the praetorians, hoping to win them over and put an end to their insane anger. And so he left the room and approached the praetorians, in an effort to discover the reason for their anger, and tried to persuade them not to act like madmen. Remaining cool and calm in this crisis and displaying the dignity of an emperor, he showed no evidence of fear or cowardice or servility.

"For me," he said, "to be murdered by you is neither important nor grievous to an old man who has received so many honors in the course of a long life. It is inevitable that every man must die someday. But for you who are supposed to be the emperor's guardians and defenders to be his murderers, and for you to stain your hands with the blood of an emperor and, what is worse, that of a fellow Roman, be sure that this is not only an act of pollution at the present but also represents a danger for you in the future. I know in my heart that I have wronged you in no way. If you are still grieved at the death of Commodus, remember that it is hardly surprising that death caught up with him. He was mortal. But if you think his death was the result of treachery, the blame does not lie with me. For you know that I am free of all suspicion on that score, and I know no more about what happened then than you do. So, if you suspect anything, bring charges against someone else. But even though Commodus is dead, you will not lack anything which can be supplied you fairly and deservedly, so long as it can be done without recourse to violence and confiscation of property."

So persuasive were his words that he had now convinced some of them; indeed, quite a few of them began to withdraw, respecting the age of their revered emperor. But while he was still talking, the bolder praetorians attacked and killed

PERTINAX, DIDIUS JULIANUS

him.[2] After they had committed this savage crime, alarmed
by what they had done and wishing to anticipate the fury of
the people, who would, they knew, be enraged by the murder, the praetorians rushed back to the camp. Shutting all the
gates and blocking the entrances, they placed sentries in the
towers and remained inside the walls to defend themselves
if the mob should attack the camp. Such was the fate of Pertinax, whose life and policies have been described above.

CHAPTER VI

WHEN the assassination of the emperor was reported
to the people, they ran about like madmen in their
grief and rage. In the grip of unreasoning fury, the mob
searched for the emperor's assassins, but were unable to find
them and take their revenge. The senators were particularly
distressed by what had happened. They considered the loss of
their benevolent father and revered protector a public disaster,
and once more there arose the fear of a tyranny, the praetorians' special delight.

But after a day or two had passed, with every man fearing
for his life, the people grew calm. Men of position went out
to their estates which were farthest from the city, to avoid
the danger of being present at the selection of the new emperor. When the praetorians saw that the people were quiet
and that no one dared to avenge the murder of the emperor,
they remained isolated inside the camp. Then, bringing forward to the walls the men with the loudest voices, they made
proclamation that the empire was for sale, promising to hand
it over to the man who offered the highest price, and promising to conduct the purchaser safely to the imperial palace
under the protection of their arms. When they made this
proclamation, the more august and respected senators, those

---
[2] March 28, 193.

BOOK TWO

who were nobly born and still wealthy, the scattered survivors of Commodus' tyranny, did not go to the wall; they had no desire to use their wealth basely and shamefully to buy the empire. But the praetorians' proposition was reported to a man named Julianus while he was giving a dinner in the late afternoon amid much drinking and carousing. This Julianus had already served a term as consul and was thought to be a very wealthy man; he was one of the Romans censured for an intemperate way of life. Then his wife and daughter and a mob of parasites persuaded him to leave his dining couch and hurry to the wall of the camp to find out what was going on. All the way to the camp they urged him to seize the prostrate empire; he had plenty of money and could outbid anyone who opposed him. And so, when they came to the wall, Julianus shouted up a promise to give the praetorians everything they wanted, assuring them that he had plenty of money, that his strongboxes were crammed with gold and silver. At the same moment the urban prefect Sulpicianus, a man of consular rank (he was the father of Pertinax' wife), came to bargain for the empire. But the praetorians refused to accept this man, afraid of his kinship with Pertinax, and fearing too that this might be a trick to avenge the emperor's murder. Lowering a ladder, they brought Julianus up to the top of the wall, for they were unwilling to open the gates until they knew how much he would pay for the empire. When he came up, Julianus promised to revive the memory of Commodus, to restore his honors, and to re-erect his statues which the senate had pulled down; he further promised to restore to the praetorians all the powers they had possessed under that emperor and to give each soldier more gold than he asked for or expected to receive. Convinced by his promises and delighted with their expectations, the guard proclaimed Julianus emperor, and, in view of his

PERTINAX, DIDIUS JULIANUS

family and his ancestry, thought it appropriate that he assume the name of Commodus. Then, raising their standards, to which pictures of Julianus had been attached, they prepared to escort the emperor to the imperial palace. After he had performed the usual imperial sacrifices in the camp, Julianus was led out under the protection of a contingent of the guard larger than normal. Because he had purchased the empire shamefully, disgracefully, and fraudulently, using force and opposing the wishes of the people, the new emperor rightly feared that the people would be hostile toward him. Therefore, under full arms and armor, the praetorians formed a phalanx so that, if necessary, they could fight. They placed their chosen emperor in the center of the formation, holding their spears and shields over their heads to protect the procession from any shower of stones hurled down from the houses. In this fashion they succeeded in conducting Julianus to the palace, as none of the people dared oppose them. No one, however, shouted the congratulations usually heard when emperors were accompanied by a formal escort; on the contrary, the people stood at a distance, shouting curses and reviling Julianus bitterly for using his wealth to purchase the empire.

It was on this occasion that the character of the praetorians was corrupted for the first time; they acquired their insatiable and disgraceful lust for money and their contempt for the sanctity of the emperor. The fact that there was no one to take action against these men who had savagely murdered their emperor, and the fact that there was no one to prevent the shameful auction and sale of the Roman empire, were the original causes of the praetorians' disgraceful and mutinous revolt at this time and also for later revolts. Their lust for gold and their contempt for their emperors increased, as did assassinations also.

CHAPTER VII

WHEN he entered into the office of emperor, Julianus immediately devoted himself to drinking and debauchery. He regarded his duties to the state as of no consequence and occupied his time in luxurious living and profligate practices. It was quickly discovered, however, that he had lied to the praetorians and deceived them, as he was unable to fulfill his promises. The truth is that he did not have as much money in his personal possession as he had pretended to have, and no money was available in the public treasuries; these had been completely exhausted by Commodus' extravagances and his lavish and endless disbursements. The praetorians, cheated of their expectations, were enraged by this insulting breach of faith; and the people, when they were aware of the praetorians' attitude, held Julianus in contempt. When the emperor appeared in public, they cursed him bitterly and taunted him for his continuous and disgraceful debauches. At the Circus Maximus, where the crowds were largest, the audience shouted insults at Julianus and called Niger defender of the empire and protector of the sacred office of emperor, begging him to come to their rescue as soon as possible, for they were subjected to unbearable indignities.

This Niger had previously served a term as consul; at the time of the events mentioned above, he was governor of Syria, then the largest and most powerful of the Roman provinces. The entire Phoenician territory and all the land as far as the Euphrates River were under Niger's command. The governor, then just past middle age, had won renown for his many brilliant exploits. He was reported to be a fair and capable man and was said to pattern his life after that of Pertinax; the Romans, consequently, had great confidence in Niger. They called for him in all the public assemblies and insulted Julianus to his face by cheering the absent Niger and offering him the empire with loud shouts.

When the attitude of the Roman people and their actions were reported to him, Niger was naturally acquiescent and believed that affairs would turn out as he wished, with no difficulty. The fact that Julianus had been deserted by the praetorians because he failed to give them the money he had promised and the fact that he was despised by the people for the shameful way in which he had bought the empire encouraged Niger to be sanguine about his chances of becoming emperor. As the first step, he summoned a few commanders and tribunes and prominent soldiers to his quarters; there he discussed the situation with them and won their support. He revealed in detail what he had heard from Rome, with the intent that, when this news was made public, it would become common knowledge to the soldiers and to the rest of the peoples of the East. He hoped to win the support of all of them without difficulty when they understood that he was not attempting to seize the empire by plotting but rather that he was going to the assistance of the people at Rome, who were begging for him to come. All the Eastern peoples flocked to his support and implored him to take charge of affairs. For the Syrian race is by nature unstable and sympathetic to any proposed change in the established order of things. In addition, the Syrians felt some affection for Niger because he ruled them mildly in all respects and staged a vast number of shows for them. They are by nature a people fond of spectacles, and the citizens of Antioch, a large and prosperous city, celebrate festivals virtually every day of the year in the city and in the surrounding area. And so, by constantly staging shows, about which they are wildly enthusiastic, and by allowing them free license to celebrate the holidays and make merry, Niger won their esteem.

CHAPTER VIII

AWARE of their high regard for him, Niger summoned the soldiers from all stations on an appointed day; after the people also had assembled, he mounted the platform erected for the purpose and addressed them as follows:

2 "The mildness of my disposition and my temperate approach in the important enterprises which I have undertaken are well known to you from of old. Never would I have come before you to discuss these matters if I were motivated solely by personal aims, by unreasonable hopes, or by the desire to realize even greater achievements. But the Romans are calling me and with unceasing cries beg me to extend to them the savior's hand and not allow an empire so illustrious, one made famous by our ancestors from the earliest times, to be

3 brought to disgraceful ruin. Just as it is rash and hasty to undertake such great projects without good cause and reason, so too is it cowardly and treasonable to hesitate when one is summoned and begged to take action. This has led me to come before you to find out what your attitude is and what you think should be done—in short, to use you as my advisers and associates in the present situation. If the issue should

4 prosper, it will work to our mutual advantage. No selfish and self-deluding hopes summon me. The Roman people call me, the Roman people, to whom the gods have given their empire and their mastery over all men. The empire too cries out to me, unsettled as it is and not yet firmly fixed in the hands of any one man. This being the situation, the safety of this course will be obvious, both from the attitude of those who are calling me and from the fact that there is no one to

5 oppose me or stand in my way. My informants in Rome say that the praetorians, who sold the empire to Julianus, are untrustworthy bodyguards because he did not pay them the

money he promised. Come now, reveal to me what your attitude is."

When he had finished speaking, the entire army and all the people there immediately hailed him as emperor and called him Augustus. They robed him in the imperial purple and provided the remaining tokens of imperial rank from whatever was available. They carried the sacred fire before their emperor and, after escorting him to the temples in Antioch, established him in his own residence, treating it no longer as a private home but as the imperial palace, for they decorated the exterior of the house with the imperial insignia.

Niger was exceedingly pleased by these developments, and believed that control of imperial affairs was firmly fixed in his hands by the attitude of the Roman people and by the enthusiasm of the Eastern peoples. When the situation became generally known, all the people on the continent of Asia lying opposite Europe came to him,[8] and every man hastened to submit to him of his own free will; embassies from all those peoples were sent to Niger at Antioch as if he were the recognized Roman emperor. The rulers and kings beyond the Tigris and Euphrates rivers sent congratulations and promised assistance if it should be needed. In return, Niger sent these rulers lavish gifts and thanked them for their support and their offers, but he assured them that he did not lack for allies. He told them that the empire was his beyond any doubt and that he intended to rule without bloodshed.

Elated by these hopes, Niger now grew negligent in attending to matters at hand. Spending his time in luxurious living, he reveled with the people of Antioch, devoting himself to shows and spectacles, and postponed his departure for

---

[8] The Propontis marked a natural dividing line between West and East. Niger, after consolidating his gains in the East, failed to extend his control of the empire by appearing personally in the West.

BOOK TWO

Rome when he should have hurried to the city at top speed. It was imperative that he visit the cities in Illyricum at the earliest possible moment and win their support before someone else did. He did not, however, release in Illyricum any report of what had happened, hoping that the army there, when it learned of these developments, would be in agreement with the entreaties of the Roman people and the attitude of the Eastern armies.

CHAPTER IX

WHILE Niger was dreaming these dreams and relying upon uncertain and unfounded hopes, what had occurred in Syria was reported to the Pannonians and the people in Illyricum, as well as to the entire military force in that area—that is, to the troops assigned to duty on the banks of the Danube and the Rhine to check barbarian incursions in those regions and defend the Roman empire. The governor of all the Pannonians (for they were at that time under one command) was a Libyan named Severus, a born administrator and a man of tremendous energy. Accustomed to a rugged life, he was physically able to endure heavy labor; mentally, he was quick to understand and quick to act once he understood. When he learned from reports that the Roman empire was dangling in the sky like a meteor for Niger and Julianus to seize, Severus, charging the former with negligence and the latter with cowardice, decided to intervene in these affairs. He had had dreams which led him to expect something like this, and his dreams were supported by oracular responses and all the signs that appear as prophecies of things to come. All these, whether they are true or false, are invariably believed when they foretell something which later actually occurs. Severus himself recorded many portents in his autobiography, and had them inscribed on his public statues also. But the last and most significant of his dreams, the one which made it clear to him that he would get all he hoped for, must not be omitted. At the time Pertinax was reported to have assumed control of the empire, Severus, after making the sacrifices and swearing the oath of allegiance to the new emperor, went back to his house at dusk and fell asleep. He dreamed that he saw a large, noble stallion adorned with the imperial trappings carrying Pertinax down the middle of the Sacred Way at Rome. But when the horse arrived at the entrance of the Forum, where, in the old days of the Republic, the popular assemblies had been held, in his dream the stallion unseated Pertinax and threw him to the ground. While Severus stood there motionless, the horse slipped under him, taking him up on his back, and bore him safely along. Then, halting in the middle of the Forum, the stallion raised Severus aloft, so that he was seen and cheered by all. And in our time a huge bronze statue depicting this dream still stood on that spot. His resolve thus strengthened, with high hopes that he was being called to the throne by divine summons, Severus made trial of the attitude of the soldiers. As the first step, he met in his quarters with a few commanders and tribunes and prominent soldiers and discussed with them the Roman empire, how it lay completely helpless because there was no man of the nobility and no man with enough ability to take control of it. He spoke with contempt of the praetorians at Rome as disloyal and false to their oath in spilling the blood of their emperor and fellow Roman, and told them that he had to go to Rome to avenge the murder of Pertinax, for he was aware that all the soldiers in Illyricum remembered the governorship of the man. When Marcus was emperor, Pertinax had won with them many victories over the Germans; after he had been appointed general and governor of the province of Illyricum, he had displayed great courage in fighting the enemy. But

BOOK TWO

at the same time he revealed his benevolence and good will toward those he ruled by his moderation and his sensible exercise of authority. For these reasons they revered his memory and were enraged at those who had treated him so savagely. Seizing this as his excuse, Severus without difficulty persuaded them to do what he wished; he pretended that he was not personally seeking the empire and did not desire power for himself, but rather that he wished to avenge the murder of so great an emperor as Pertinax. Although the men of those regions have huge and powerful bodies and are skillful and murderous in battle, they are dull of wit and slow to realize that they are being deceived. Hence they believed Severus when he said that he was enraged and wished to avenge the murder of Pertinax; and, putting themselves in his hands, they made him emperor and turned the control of the empire over to him. Since he now knew the attitude of the Pannonians, he reported these events to the neighboring provinces and to the rulers of all the northern nations under Roman control; he convinced them by lavish promises and the expectation of great rewards, and easily won their support. He was surely the most accomplished of all men in pretending to pledge his good will, but he never kept his sworn word if it proved necessary for him to break it; he lied whenever it was advantageous to him, and his tongue said many things which his heart did not mean.

CHAPTER X

SEVERUS sent letters to all the soldiers in Illyricum and to their officers and won their support. After assembling the troops from all stations, he assumed as his names both Severus and Pertinax, hoping that this would endear him not only to the people in Illyricum but also to the Romans because of their memories of that emperor. He then called

PERTINAX, DIDIUS JULIANUS

the soldiers together on the assembly ground and, mounting a platform erected for him, addressed them as follows:

"The faith and reverence which you have for the gods, by whom you swear, and the respect which you have for your emperors, whom you esteem, you have made abundantly clear by your rage at the acts of the praetorians in Rome, who are more suited for parades than for battles. And now, because you ask it, although I never before entertained such a hope (you know my loyalty to the emperors), it is my duty to undertake and successively resolve these matters which have your approval. I must not allow the Roman empire to lie helpless, that empire which, to the end of Marcus' reign, was administered with reverence and appeared to be august and awesome. Under Commodus, however, the empire underwent a change, and yet, even if it did suffer somewhat at his hands because of his youth, all was forgiven him because of his noble birth and the memory of his father. And the truth is that there was more reason to pity than to despise him for his errors, in that we attributed most of what happened not to him personally but to the parasites who swarmed around him and to his advisers and accomplices in his irregular acts. But when the empire came into the hands of that revered elder statesman Pertinax, the memory of whose courage and service to the state is still firmly fixed in our hearts, the praetorians not only did not protect their emperor, but went so far as to murder that illustrious man. And now some fellow has disgracefully purchased the empire and its vast expanse of land and sea; as you have heard, he is hated by the people and no longer trusted by the disillusioned praetorians. Even if they loved him and intended to support him, you outnumber them and are superior in courage. You have trained under actual combat conditions in your continuous skirmishes with the barbarians, and you are accustomed to endure all kinds of labor. Ignoring heat and cold, you cross

BOOK TWO

frozen rivers on the ice; you do not drink water from wells, but water you have dug yourself. You have also trained by fighting with animals, and, all in all, you have won so distinguished a reputation for bravery that no one could stand
6 against you. Toil is the true test of the soldier, not easy living, and those luxury-loving sots would not face your battle cry, much less your battle line. But if any one of you is concerned about affairs in Syria, he may judge how feeble the effort is there and how slight the hope of success by the fact that these men have not dared to venture beyond their own borders and were not bold enough to plan for a journey to Rome. There they remain, content, believing that this temporary taste of living in luxury represents the total profit to them
7 of this firmly established empire. The truth is that the Syrians are suited only to games and childish banter. This is especially true of those who live in Antioch, who are reported to be highly enthusiastic supporters of Niger. But the rest of the provinces and cities have up to now found no one worthy of the imperial throne, and, because no man has appeared who will rule with courage and use sound administrative practices, it is evident that they are only pretending to support
8 that fellow. But if they should learn that the army of Illyricum has already made its choice, and if they should hear our name, which is not unknown or without honor among them, because of our term as governor of Syria, know well, I say, that they will not find fault with me for delay or cowardice, nor will they elect to stand and face your bravery and your battle prowess, for they are greatly inferior to you in size of body, in endurance of hardship, and in close-quarter combat.
9 Let us therefore occupy Rome before they do it; that city is the seat of the empire. By establishing our headquarters in Rome, we shall manage the rest easily, putting our trust in divine prophecies and our reliance in your strength and your arms."

PERTINAX, DIDIUS JULIANUS

After Severus had finished speaking, the soldiers shouted his praises, calling him Augustus and Pertinax, and displaying the utmost zeal and enthusiasm for him.

CHAPTER XI

WITHOUT delay and waste of time, Severus ordered them to get ready only as much gear as each could conveniently carry, and announced his decision to depart for Rome. He distributed money to the troops and issued supplies for the journey. With prodigious effort, he sped on his way, stopping nowhere and allowing no time for rest except for the brief periods necessary to enable the soldiers to recover from the rigorous march. He shared personally in their hardships, sleeping in an ordinary army tent and eating and drinking whatever was available to all; on no occasion did he make use of imperial luxuries or comforts. As a result, he enjoyed even greater popularity among the troops; respecting him not only for sharing their hardships but also for overcoming all difficulties, they carried out his orders with enthusiasm.

After crossing Pannonia, Severus came to the mountains of Italy; outstripping the news of his approach, he appeared in person to the people there before they had heard that he was emperor or that he was on his way to Rome. The cities of Italy regarded the approach of this formidable army with apprehension. The men of Italy, long unused to arms and war, were devoted to farming and peaceful pursuits. As long as Roman affairs were governed by Republican principles and the senate selected the generals who took charge of military affairs, all the Italians were under arms, and controlled the lands and the seas, waging wars with Greeks and barbarians. There was no place on earth, no place under heaven, to which the Romans did not extend the borders of their

BOOK TWO

5 empire. From the time when Augustus assumed control of the government, however, the *princeps* freed the Italians from the necessity of working and of bearing arms; establishing forts and camps for the defense of the empire, he stationed mercenaries in these to serve as a defensive bulwark on the frontiers. The empire was further protected by great barriers
6 of rivers and mountains and impassable deserts. When the people of Italy learned that Severus was approaching with a huge army, they were understandably dismayed by the unexpectedness of this development. Not daring to oppose him or try to stop him, they took up laurel branches and went out to meet him, welcoming him with open gates. Delaying only to secure good omens and say a few words to the people, Severus hurried on to Rome.
7 When these developments were reported to Julianus, he was in despair because of what he had heard about the size and the power of the army of Illyricum, because of his lack of faith in the Roman people, who hated him, and because of his lack of confidence in the praetorians, whom he had swindled. Still, he collected his own money and that of his friends, appropriated what was left in the public and temple treasuries, and undertook to distribute this sum among the
8 praetorians in an effort to purchase their good will. But in spite of the fact that they received large amounts of money, the praetorians were in no way grateful to the emperor; they felt that he was not giving them a bonus but only paying them what he owed them.

Although his friends advised him to lead out the army and seize the passes of the Alps, Julianus did nothing. The Alps are very tall mountains—there are none like them in our part of the world; they surround Italy like a wall and are her first line of defense. This is yet another piece of good fortune which Nature has provided the Italians, an impregnable barrier across their entire northern frontier, for the Alps

PERTINAX, DIDIUS JULIANUS

extend unbroken from the Tyrrhenian to the Adriatic Sea. But Julianus, as I have said, did not dare to venture forth from Rome. He did, however, send a message to the praetorians, begging them to take up arms, practice their drills, and dig trenches to defend the city. In the city he made what preparations he could for the battle with Severus. All the elephants used by the Romans in parades were trained to carry men and towers on their backs. It was hoped that the elephants would terrify the troops from Illyricum and stampede the enemy cavalry when these huge beasts, which the horses had never seen before, appeared on the field. The whole city was training in arms and preparing for battle.

CHAPTER XII

WHILE Julianus' troops were delaying and preparing for battle, word came that Severus was approaching. Dividing most of his army into small bands, Severus ordered them to slip into the city unnoticed. Spreading out along all the roads into Rome, many by day, but even more by night, entered the city unobserved, in civilian disguise, with their weapons concealed. The enemy was thus already in the city while Julianus was hesitating, unaware of what was happening. When the people learned of these developments, they were in complete confusion; fearing the army of Severus, they pretended to support his cause, charging Julianus with cowardice and Niger with hesitation and sloth. But when they heard that Severus was in Rome, the people were thunderstruck. Julianus, dumb and witless, did not know how to handle the situation. Ordering the senate to convene, he sent a letter to Severus in which he proposed peace and, proclaiming him emperor, made him his colleague in governing the empire. The senate voted its approval of these proposals; but when it was obvious that Julianus was terror-stricken and in

BOOK TWO

4 despair, all the senators immediately abandoned him for Severus. After two or three days had passed, the senators, aware that Severus was in Rome, contemptuous of Julianus, entered the senate house at the order of the consuls, the officials who took charge at Rome when the affairs of the empire
5 were in confusion. After convening, the senate consulted about what should be done in the present emergency. Meanwhile, Julianus was still in the imperial palace bewailing the disaster that had befallen him and pleading to be allowed to resign as emperor and turn the entire power over to Severus.
6 When the senate learned that Julianus was cowering in fear and that the Praetorian Guard had deserted him in terror of Severus, that body voted to take the empire from Julianus and proclaim Severus sole emperor. They therefore sent to Severus an embassy made up of the chief officials and the most distinguished senators to hand over to him all the
7 imperial honors. A tribune was sent to kill Julianus, that cowardly and wretched old man who had in this way purchased with his own money his miserable death.

CHAPTER XIII

DESERTED by all, Julianus was found weeping disgracefully and was killed. When he learned of the senate's action and the death of Julianus, Severus, encouraged to hope for greater success, used a trick to seize and hold prisoner the Praetorian Guard, the murderers of Pertinax. He quietly sent private letters to the tribunes and centurions, promising them rich rewards if they would persuade the praetorians in Rome to submit and obey the emperor's or-
2 ders. He also sent an open letter to the praetorian camp, directing the soldiers to leave their weapons behind in the camp and come forth unarmed, as was the custom when they escorted the emperor to the sacrifices or to the celebration of

PERTINAX, DIDIUS JULIANUS

a festival. He further ordered them to swear the oath of allegiance in his name and to present themselves with good expectations of continuing to serve as the emperor's bodyguard. Trusting these orders and persuaded by their tribunes, the praetorians left their arms behind and appeared from the camp in holiday uniform, carrying laurel branches. Arriving at Severus' camp, they sent word that they were at the assembly ground where the emperor had ordered them to muster for a welcoming address. The praetorians moved toward the emperor as he was mounting the speaking platform; then, at a given signal, they were all seized while cheering him in unison. Prior orders had been issued to Severus' soldiers to surround the praetorians, now their enemy, at the moment when they were standing with their eyes fixed in expectant attention upon the emperor; they were not, however, to wound or strike any member of the guard. Severus ordered his troops to hold the praetorians in a tight ring of steel, believing that they would not resist, since they were only a few unarmed men, fearful of wounds, confronted by an armed host. When he had them netted like fish in his circle of weapons, like prisoners of war, the enraged emperor shouted in a loud voice:

"You see by what has happened that we are superior to you in intelligence, in size of army, and in number of supporters. Surely you were easily trapped, captured without a struggle. It is in my power to do with you what I wish when I wish. Helpless and prostrate, you lie before us now, victims of our might. But if one looks for a punishment equal to the crimes you have committed, it is impossible to find a suitable one. You murdered your revered and benevolent old emperor, the man whom it was your sworn duty to protect. The empire of the Roman people, eternally respected, which our forefathers obtained by their valiant courage or inherited because of their noble birth, this empire you shamefully and

BOOK TWO

7 disgracefully sold for silver as if it were your personal property. But you were unable to defend the man whom you yourselves had chosen as emperor. No, you betrayed him like the cowards you are. For these monstrous acts and crimes you deserve a thousand deaths, if one wished to do to you what you have earned. You see clearly what it is right you should suffer. But I will be merciful. I will not butcher you.

8 My hands shall not do what your hands did. But I say that it is in no way fit or proper for you to continue to serve as the emperor's bodyguard, you who have violated your oath and stained your hands with the blood of your emperor and fellow Roman, betraying the trust placed in you and the security offered by your protection. Still, compassion leads me to spare your lives and your persons. But I order the soldiers who have you surrounded to cashier you, to strip off any military uniform or equipment you are wearing, and

9 drive you off naked. And I order you to get yourselves as far from the city of Rome as is humanly possible, and I promise you and I swear it on solemn oath and I proclaim it publicly that if any one of you is found within a hundred miles of Rome, he shall pay for it with his head."

10 After he had issued these orders, the soldiers from Illyricum rushed forward and stripped from the praetorians their short ceremonial swords inlaid with gold and silver; next, they ripped off belts, uniforms, and any military insignia they

11 were wearing, and sent them off naked. The praetorians had to submit to this treatment, since they were betrayed and taken by a trick. Indeed, what else could they do—a few naked men against so many fully armed soldiers? They left then, lamenting their fate, and, although they accepted with gratitude the safe-conduct granted them, they bitterly regretted that they had left the camp without arms and had been trapped in this humiliating and high-handed fashion.

12 The circumstances of the situation led Severus to use another stratagem. Fearing that, after they had been cashiered from

PERTINAX, DIDIUS JULIANUS

the service, the praetorians might rush back to the camp and snatch up their arms, the emperor sent ahead, by other streets and ways, men picked for their demonstrated courage; these men were to reach the camp ahead of the praetorians, seize the arms there, and shut out the guards if they came to the camp.

Such was the punishment suffered by the murderers of Pertinax.

CHAPTER XIV

THEN Severus entered Rome with all the rest of his army under arms: his presence in the city brought fear and panic to the Romans because of his achievements, so daring and favored by fortune. The people and the senate, carrying laurel branches, received him, the foremost of men and emperors, who had accomplished great deeds without bloodshed or difficulty. Everything about the man was extraordinary, but especially outstanding were his shrewd judgment, his endurance of toils, and his spirit of bold optimism in everything he did. Then, after the people had welcomed him with cheers and the senate had saluted him at the city gates, Severus went into the temple of Jupiter and offered sacrifices; after sacrificing in the rest of the shrines in accord with imperial practice, he entered the palace. On the following day he went to the senate and addressed all the senators in a speech that was very mild in tone and full of promises of good things for the future. Greeting them collectively and individually, he told them that he had come to avenge the murder of Pertinax and assured them that his reign would mark the reintroduction of senatorial rule. No man would be put to death or have his property confiscated without a trial; he would not tolerate informers; he would bring unlimited prosperity to his subjects; he intended to imitate Marcus' reign in every way; and he would assume not only

BOOK TWO

4 the name but also the manner and approach of Pertinax. By this speech he won a good opinion for himself among most of the senators, and they believed his promises. But some of the older senators knew the true character of the man, and said privately that he was indeed a man of great cunning, who knew how to manage things shrewdly; they further said that he was very skillful at deceit and at feigning anything and everything; and, moreover, he always did what was of benefit and profit to his own interests. The truth of these observations was later demonstrated by what the man actually did.

5 After spending a short time in Rome, during which he made generous gifts to the people, staged shows, and rewarded his soldiers lavishly, he chose for service in the imperial bodyguard, to replace the praetorians he had dismissed, the best-qualified soldiers from his army. He then set out for
6 the East. Since Niger was still delaying and wasting time in luxurious living in Antioch, Severus wished to surprise him before he was prepared. He therefore ordered his soldiers to be ready to march, and collected recruits everywhere, calling up the young men from the cities of Italy and enrolling them in the army. All the units of the army he had left behind in Illyricum were directed to march into Thrace and join
7 him there. He fitted out a naval unit; manning with heavily armed troops all the triremes in Italy, he sent these off too. He got ready a large and powerful force with incredible speed, aware that he would need a large army to operate against Niger and the entire continent lying opposite Europe.

CHAPTER XV

SEVERUS made preparations for the war with great care. A thorough and cautious man, he had his doubts about the army in Britain, which was large and very powerful, manned by excellent soldiers. Britain was then under the command of Albinus, a man of the senatorial order who had been reared in luxury on money inherited from his ancestors. Severus, wishing to gain the friendship of this man, deceived him by a trick; he feared that Albinus, having strong stimuli to encourage him to seize the throne, and made bold by his ancestry and wealth, a powerful army, and his popularity among the Romans, might seize the empire and occupy Rome while Severus was busy with affairs in the East. And so he deceived the man by pretending to do him honor. Albinus, conceited and somewhat naïve in his judgment, really believed the many things which Severus swore on oath in his letters. Severus appointed him Caesar, to anticipate his hope and desire for a share of the imperial power. He wrote Albinus the friendliest of letters, deceitful, of course, in which he begged the man to devote his attention to the welfare of the empire. He wrote him that the situation required a man of the nobility in the prime of life; he himself was old and afflicted with gout, and his sons were still very young. Believing Severus, Albinus gratefully accepted the honor, delighted to be getting what he wanted without fighting and without risk. After making these same proposals to the senate, to increase their faith in him, Severus ordered coins to be struck bearing his likeness, and he increased the favor he had won by erecting statues of himself and assuming the rest of the imperial honors. When he had, by his cunning, arranged matters securely with respect to Albinus and consequently had nothing to fear from Britain, the emperor, accompanied by the entire army of Illyricum, set out against Niger, convinced that he had arranged to his own advantage everything affecting his reign.

Where he halted on his march, what he said in each city, the portents that seemed to appear by divine foresight, the countries and conflicts, the number of men on each side who

BOOK TWO

7 fell in battle, all these have been recorded fully enough by numerous historians and poets who have made the life of Severus the subject of their entire work. But it is my intent to write a chronological account of the exploits of many emperors over a period of seventy years, exploits about which I have knowledge from personal experience. Therefore I shall record the most significant and distinguished of Severus' achievements in the order in which they occurred, not selecting the favorable ones in order to flatter him, as did the writers of his own day; but, on the other hand, I shall omit nothing worth telling or worth remembering.

BOOK THREE

SEPTIMIUS SEVERUS

CHAPTER I

THE death of Pertinax, the killing of Julianus, the entrance of Severus into Rome, and his expedition against Niger have all been described in the preceding book. When Niger learned that Severus had occupied Rome, had been proclaimed emperor by the senate, and was leading the entire army of Illyricum against him, supported by the rest of the infantry and a naval unit as well, he was greatly disturbed by these unexpected developments. He sent orders to the governors of the Eastern provinces to keep a close guard on all the passes and harbors. He also sent word to the king of the Parthians, to the king of the Armenians, and to the king of the Atrenians, asking for aid. The Armenian king replied that he would not form an alliance with anyone, but was ready to defend his own lands if Severus should attack him now. The Parthian king, on the other hand, said that he would order his governors to collect troops—the customary practice whenever it was necessary to raise an army, as they have no standing army and do not hire mercenaries. Barsemius, king of the Atrenians, sent a contingent of native arch-

BOOK THREE

4 ers to aid Niger. The rest of his army Niger collected from the troops stationed in those areas. Most of the citizens of Antioch, especially the young men, who, in their instability, were enthusiastic supporters of Niger, offered themselves for military service, acting more in haste than in wisdom. Niger ordered that the narrow passes and cliffs of the Taurus Mountains should be defended by strong walls and fortifications, believing that an impassable mountain range would be a powerful protection for the highways of the East. The Taurus Mountains, which lie between Cappadocia and Cilicia, mark
5 the dividing line between the East and the West. Niger also sent an army to occupy Byzantium in Thrace, at that time a large and prosperous city rich in men and money. Located at the narrowest part of the Propontic Gulf, Byzantium grew immensely wealthy from its marine revenues, both tolls and fish; the city owned much fertile land, too, and realized a
6 very handsome profit from all these sources. Niger wished to have this city under his control because it was very strong, but especially because he hoped to be able to prevent any crossing from Europe and Asia by way of the Propontic Gulf. Byzantium was surrounded by a huge, strong wall of millstones cut to rectangular shape and fitted so skillfully that it was impossible to determine where the courses were joined;
7 the entire wall appeared to be a single block of stone. Even now the surviving ruins of this wall are enough to make the viewer marvel both at the technical skill of the original builders and the might of those who finally destroyed it.

Niger was thus acting, as he believed, with the greatest possible foresight to guarantee the utmost security.

CHAPTER II

SEVERUS, in the meantime, pressed on with his army at top speed, halting for neither rest nor refreshment. Having learned that Byzantium, which he knew was defended

SEPTIMIUS SEVERUS

by the strongest of city walls, had been occupied by Niger, Severus ordered his army to march to Cyzicus. The governor of Asia at that time was the general Aemilianus, to whom Niger had entrusted the military preparations in that province. When he learned that the army of Severus was approaching, Aemilianus marched toward Cyzicus at the head of his entire army, which included both the troops he had enrolled himself and those sent to him by Niger. When the two armies met, savage battles were fought in those regions; the army of Severus conquered, and the soldiers of Niger, put to flight, were routed and slaughtered. Thus the hopes of the East were shattered, while the hopes of the Illyrians soared.

There are those who say that Niger's cause, immediately betrayed by Aemilianus, was doomed from the start, and they cite two reasons for that general's action. Some say that the governor plotted against Niger because he was jealous and angry that his successor as governor of Syria was about to become his superior as emperor and tyrant. Others, however, say that he was forced to betray Niger by his own children, who urgently begged him to do so in order to insure their own safety; for Severus, finding Aemilianus' children at Rome, had seized them and was holding them under guard. Nor was he the first to make use of this extremely foresighted stratagem. It was Commodus' practice to keep in custody the children of the governors of the provinces in order to have pledges of their loyalty and good will. Severus, familiar with this practice, when he was made emperor and Julianus was still alive, grew anxious about his children. Sending for them in secret, he had them brought to him from Rome to prevent their falling into the hands of someone else. When he came to Rome, Severus gathered up the children of the governors and those who occupied positions of importance in the East and all Asia and held them in custody; these children he kept so that the governors might be led to be-

BOOK THREE

tray Niger in fear for the safety of their children, or, if they continued to favor his cause, envisaging the agony they would suffer if their children were killed, they might do something to protect them.

6 After the defeat at Cyzicus, the troops of Niger scattered far and wide; some fled into the mountains of Armenia, others into Galatia and Asia, hoping to reach the Taurus Mountains before the soldiers of Severus and take refuge behind the fortifications there. Meanwhile the army of Severus pressed on, passing through Cyzicus and advancing into neighboring Bithynia.

7 When the report of Severus' victory was made public, dissension immediately arose in the cities of all those provinces, not so much because of affection or good will toward the warring emperors but from mutual jealousy, envy, and hatred, together with indignation over the slaughter of their

8 fellow citizens. This is an ancient failing of the Greeks; the constant organizing of factions against each other and their eagerness to bring about the downfall of those who seem superior to them have ruined Greece. Their ancient quarrels and internal feuds had made them easy prey to the Macedonians and slaves to the Romans, and this curse of jealousy and envy has been handed down to the flourishing Greek

9 cities of our own day. Immediately after these events in Cyzicus, the Nicomedians in Bithynia announced their support of Severus; they sent envoys to him, welcomed his army, and promised to supply all his needs. The Niceans, on the other hand, because they hated the Nicomedians, welcomed the army of Niger, both the fugitives who came to them and

10 the troops sent by Niger to defend Bithynia. Then the soldiers on each side rushed forth from the two cities as if from regular army camps and crashed together; after a savage struggle, the supporters of Severus won a decisive victory. The adherents of Niger who survived the battle fled from

those regions and poured into the Taurus Mountains, where they blocked the passes and held the fortifications under guard. But Niger, leaving a force which he considered adequate for the defense of these barricades, hurried off to Antioch to collect troops and money.

CHAPTER III

PASSING through Bithynia and Galatia, the army of Severus swept into Cappadocia; there it halted and put the defense works under siege. This was no small undertaking, however: the narrow rough road made an approach very difficult; and Niger's soldiers, fighting back bravely, stood upon the battlements and hurled stones down on the attackers. Thus a few defenders easily held off a great number of attackers, for the narrow approach was protected on one side by a lofty mountain and on the other by a steep cliff which served as the channel of a waterfall formed by mountain streams. All these natural defenses had been utilized by Niger to block Severus' approach from any direction.

While these things were happening in Cappadocia, where mutual jealousy and enmity were general, the Laodiceans in Syria revolted from Niger because they hated the people of Antioch, and the people of Tyre in Phoenicia revolted because they hated the people of Berytus. When they learned that Niger was in headlong flight, the people of these two cities decided to risk stripping him of his honors and publicly proclaimed their support of Severus. Niger learned of this action while he was in Antioch, and although up to this time he had been quite mild, he was now justifiably angered by their insolent defection and sent against them his Moroccan javelin men and some of the archers too, ordering them to kill everyone they met, loot the two cities, and burn them to the ground. The Moroccans are the most brutal and sav-

BOOK THREE

age men in the world and are wholly indifferent to death or danger. Taking the Laodiceans by surprise, they destroyed the city and slaughtered the inhabitants. Then they hurried on to Tyre and, after much looting and killing, burned the whole city.

6 While these events were taking place in Syria and Niger was collecting an army, the troops of Severus pitched camp and besieged the fortifications in the Taurus Mountains. The soldiers were disheartened and discouraged, however; the defenses, protected by a mountain and a cliff, were strong 7 and difficult to approach. But when the army of Severus was about to abandon the siege and their opponents believed that their position was impregnable, rain suddenly fell in torrents during the night, and much snow along with it. (The winters are severe in Cappadocia and especially so in the Taurus Mountains.) A large and violent stream of water now poured down on the fortifications, which blocked the regular stream bed and checked the torrent; hence the current became deep and strong. Then Nature prevailed over man's handiwork, and the wall was unable to hold back the stream. The wall did briefly withstand the pressure of the water on its joints, but finally the foundations, which had been constructed hastily and without the usual care, were undermined by the torrent and the wall collapsed. The whole fortification was exposed, and the stream, leveling the area, 8 breached the defense works. When those on guard at the barricade saw what had happened, they feared that they would be surrounded and trapped by the rushing flood; abandoning their posts, they fled, since there was no longer anything to keep the enemy out. Delighted by this turn of events, the troops of Severus rejoiced, believing that they were under the guidance of divine providence; when they saw the guards fleeing in all directions they crossed the Taurus Mountains without difficulty or opposition and marched into Cilicia.

CHAPTER IV

WHEN he learned what had happened, Niger collected a huge army, but one unused to battle and toil, and marched out in haste. A large number of men, especially the youths of Antioch, presented themselves for service in the campaign, risking their lives for him. The enthusiasm of his army naturally encouraged Niger, but his soldiers were much inferior to the Illyrians in skill and courage. Both armies marched out to a flat, sweeping plain near a bay called Issus; there a ridge of hills forms a natural theater on this plain, and a broad beach slopes down to the sea, as if Nature had constructed a stadium for a battle. It was there, they say, that Darius fought his last and greatest battle with Alexander and was defeated and captured when the West defeated the East.[1] Even today a memorial and a monument of the victory remain: a city on the ridge, called Alexandria, and a bronze statue from which the region gets its name.

The armies of Severus and Niger not only met at that historic spot but the outcome of the battle was the same. The armies pitched camp opposite each other toward evening, and spent a sleepless night, anxious and afraid. With each of the generals urging his men on, the armies advanced to the attack at sunrise, fighting with savage fury, as if this were destined to be the final and decisive battle and Fortune would there choose one of them as emperor. After the battle had continued for a long time with terrible slaughter, and the rivers which flowed through the plain were pouring more blood than water into the sea, the rout of the forces of the East began. Driving Niger's battered troops before them,

---

[1] Herodian is in error on all points here. Issus was neither the last nor the most decisive battle in the Persian campaign, and Darius was never captured alive by Alexander.

BOOK THREE

the Illyrians forced some of the fugitives into the sea; pursuing the rest as they rushed to the ridges, they slaughtered the fugitives, as well as a large number of men from the nearby towns and farms who had gathered to watch the battle from a safe vantage point.

6 Mounting a good horse, Niger fled with a few companions to Antioch. There he found the survivors of the rout, weeping and wailing, mourning the loss of sons and brothers. Niger now fled from Antioch in despair. Discovered hiding in the outskirts of the city, he was beheaded by the pursuing horsemen [A.D. 194].

7 Such was the fate Niger suffered, and he paid the penalty he deserved for his negligence and indecision. In other respects, however, they say that he was in no way despicable either as emperor or as man. Having eliminated Niger, Severus now put to death without mercy all the man's friends, whether they had supported him by choice or by necessity. When he learned that some of Niger's soldiers had managed to escape across the Tigris River and that, fearing the emperor, they were joining forces with the barbarians there, he induced a few to return, by granting them full pardon, but the majority of the fugitives remained in that alien land.

8 Thereafter, the battle tactics of the barbarians in those regions were much more effective against the close-quarter fighting of the Romans. Formerly, the barbarians did not use swords and spears in battle; they fought only as mounted archers. And instead of wearing full body armor, they rode in light, loose-fitting uniforms. Their method of fighting was

9 to flee on horseback and shoot their arrows behind them. But since the Roman fugitives were all soldiers, and there were technicians among those who elected to settle permanently across the Tigris River, the barbarians learned from them both the use and the manufacture of arms.

CHAPTER V

AFTER settling Eastern affairs in what he thought was the most advantageous way, Severus wished to take the field immediately against the Atrenian king and invade Parthia also, charging both of these kings with friendship for Niger. He put off these projects until later, however, wishing to seize the Roman empire first and make it secure for himself and his sons. Even though Niger had been eliminated, Severus considered Albinus still a menace. He now heard that this man, delighted with the title of Caesar, was acting more and more like an emperor; he was informed also that a great many men, particularly the most distinguished senators, were writing public and private letters to the Caesar, trying to persuade him to come to Rome while Severus was absent and occupied elsewhere. The fact is that the aristocracy much preferred Albinus as emperor because he belonged to a noble family and was reputed to have a mild nature. When he learned of these developments, Severus declined to initiate open hostility against Albinus and start a war with him since he lacked a reasonable excuse for such action. He thought it best to try to eliminate his Caesar by tricking him without warning. He therefore sent his most trusted imperial messengers to Britain with secret orders to hand Albinus the dispatches openly if they were admitted to his presence. They were then to ask him to meet them privately to receive secret instructions; when Albinus agreed to this and his bodyguards were not present, the messengers were to attack him without warning and cut him down. Severus provided them with deadly poisons so that, if the opportunity presented itself, they might persuade one of his cooks or cupbearers to administer a dose in secret. Albinus' advisers, however, were suspicious of the emperor's messengers,

BOOK THREE

and warned him to be on his guard against this cunning schemer. Severus' actions against Niger's governors had seriously damaged his reputation; after forcing them through their children to betray Niger, as has been related above, and after making good use of their assistance, he put them to death with their children after he had got from them everything he wanted. His actions on this occasion clearly revealed Severus' despicable character. The efforts of Severus now led Albinus to increase the size of his bodyguard. None of the emperor's men was admitted into the Caesar's presence until he had first been stripped and searched for concealed weapons. Now when the messengers from Severus arrived, they handed over the dispatches to Albinus openly and asked him to retire with them to receive secret orders. But Albinus, suspicious, had the men seized, and, putting them to torture privately, discovered the entire plot; after killing the messengers, he prepared to resist his revealed enemy.

CHAPTER VI

WHEN he was informed of what had occurred, Severus took effective and energetic action; by nature quick to anger, he no longer concealed his hostility toward Albinus. Calling together the entire army, he spoke to them as follows:

"Let no one charge us with capricious inconsistency in our actions against Albinus, and let no one think that I am disloyal to this alleged friend or lacking in feeling toward him. We gave this man everything, even a share of the established empire, a thing which a man would hardly do for his own brother. Indeed, I bestowed upon him that which you entrusted to me alone. Surely Albinus has shown little gratitude for the many benefits I have lavished upon him. Now

SEPTIMIUS SEVERUS

he is collecting an army to take up arms against us, scornful of your valor and indifferent to his pledge of good faith to me, wishing in his insatiable greed to seize at the risk of disaster that which he has already received in part without war and without bloodshed, showing no respect for the gods by whom he has often sworn, and counting as worthless the labors you performed on our joint behalf with such courage and devotion to duty. In what you accomplished, he also had 4 a share, and he would have had an even greater share of the honor you gained for us both if he had only kept his word. For, just as it is unfair to initiate wrong actions, so also it is cowardly to make no defense against unjust treatment. Now when we took the field against Niger, we had reasons for our hostility, not entirely logical, perhaps, but inevitable. We did not hate him because he had seized the empire after it was already ours, but rather each one of us, motivated by an equal desire for glory, sought the empire for himself alone, when it was still in dispute and lay prostrate before all. But Albinus has violated his pledges and broken his 5 oaths, and although he received from me that which a man normally gives only to his son, he has chosen to be hostile rather than friendly and belligerent instead of peaceful. And just as we were generous to him previously and showered fame and honor upon him, so let us now punish him with our arms for his treachery and cowardice. His army, small 6 and island-bred, will not stand against your might. For you, who by your valor and readiness to act on your own behalf have been victorious in many battles and have gained control of the entire East, how can you fail to emerge victorious with the greatest of ease when you have so large a number of allies and when virtually the entire army is here. Whereas they, by contrast, are few in number and lack a brave and competent general to lead them. Who does not know Al- 7 binus' effeminate nature? Who does not know that his way

BOOK THREE

of life has prepared him more for the chorus than for the battlefield? Let us therefore go forth against him with confidence, relying on our customary zeal and valor, with the gods as our allies, gods against whom he has acted impiously in breaking his oaths, and let us be mindful of the victories we have won, victories which that man ridicules."

8 When Severus had finished speaking, the entire army called Albinus enemy and shouted their approval of Severus, promising him their wholehearted support; as a result, he was inspired even more and encouraged to anticipate greater things. After making generous gifts to the soldiers, Severus 9 publicly announced his expedition against Albinus. He also sent troops to continue the siege of Byzantium, which was still under blockade because the soldiers of Niger had fled there. At a later date Byzantium was captured as a result of famine, and the entire city was razed. Stripped of its theaters and baths and, indeed, of all adornments, the city, now only a village, was given to the Perinthians to be subject to them; in the same way Antioch was given to the Laodiceans. Severus made available a huge sum of money for rebuilding 10 the cities destroyed by Niger's soldiers. The emperor himself set out on the march, scorning heat and cold alike, and gave the army no respite for holidays or rest. Often when he was journeying through very high and very cold mountains, the emperor strode along bareheaded through rain and snow, setting an example of courage and constancy for his soldiers, who endured hardships not only from fear and from training but also in imitation of their emperor. Severus sent a general ahead with a unit of soldiers to seize the passes of the Alps and guard the approaches to Italy.

CHAPTER VII

WHEN it was reported that Severus was not merely threatening to come but would soon appear in person, Albinus was in a state of complete confusion amid the negligence and revelry. Crossing over to the mainland of Gaul opposite Britain, he established his headquarters there. He then sent messages to the governors of the provinces ordering them to provide food and money for his army. Some obeyed and sent supplies, to their own destruction, since they suffered for it later; those who did not obey him saved themselves, more by luck than good judgment. The outcome of the affair and the fortunes of war determined the wisdom of each decision. When the army of Severus came to Gaul, a few minor skirmishes occurred here and there, but the final battle was fought near the large and prosperous city of Lugdunum [Lyon]. Albinus shut himself up in that city, remaining behind when he sent the army out to do battle. A major engagement developed, and for a long time each side's chances of victory were equal, for in courage and ruthlessness the soldiers from Britain were in no way inferior to the soldiers from Illyria. When these two magnificent armies were locked in combat, it was no easy matter to put either one to flight. As some contemporary historians recorded— saying it not to curry favor but in the interests of accuracy —the division of the army stationed opposite the sector where Severus and his command were fighting proved far superior; the emperor slipped from his horse and fled, managing to escape by throwing off the imperial cloak. But while the soldiers from Britain were pursuing the Illyrians, chanting paeans of praise as if they were already victorious, they say that Laetus, one of Severus' generals, appeared with the troops under his command fresh and not yet committed in

BOOK THREE

4 the battle. The historians accuse Laetus of watching the progress of the battle and deliberately waiting, holding his troops out of the fighting and appearing only after he was informed that Severus had been beaten. The aftermath of the affair substantiates the charge that Laetus coveted the empire himself. Later, when Severus had set everything straight and was living an orderly life, he gave generous rewards to the rest of his commanders, but Laetus alone he put to death, as seems reasonable under the circumstances, considering the

5 general's past performances. All this happened at a much later date, however. On this occasion, when Laetus appeared with fresh troops, as has been related above, Severus' soldiers, taking heart, wrapped the emperor in the imperial

6 cloak again and mounted him on his horse. But Albinus' soldiers, thinking that the victory was theirs, now found themselves in disorder when this powerful and as yet uncommitted army suddenly attacked; after a brief resistance they broke and ran. When the rout became general, Severus' soldiers pursued and slaughtered the fugitives until they drove them into Lugdunum. Each contemporary historian has recorded to suit his own purpose the actual number of

7 those killed and captured on each side. The emperor's troops captured Lugdunum and burned it. When they caught Albinus they cut off his head and sent it to Severus [A.D. 197]. The emperor thus won two magnificent victories, one in the East and one in the West. No battles and no victories can be compared to those of Severus, and no army to the size of his army; there are no comparable uprisings among nations, or total number of campaigns, or length and speed of marches.

8 Momentous indeed were the battles of Caesar against Pompey, when Roman fought Roman; equally momentous were the battles fought by Augustus against Antony and the sons of Pompey, and the struggles of Sulla and Marius at an earlier date, in the Roman civil and foreign wars. But here is one

SEPTIMIUS SEVERUS

man who overthrew three emperors after they were already ruling, and got the upper hand over the praetorians by a trick: he succeeded in killing Julianus, the man in the imperial palace; Niger, who had previously governed the people of the East and was saluted as emperor by the Roman people; and Albinus, who had already been awarded the honor and authority of Caesar. He prevailed over them all by his courage. It is not possible to name another like Severus.

Such was the fate suffered by Albinus, who was stripped of the honor which destroyed him after a brief time.

CHAPTER VIII

THEN the angry emperor took vengeance upon Albinus' friends at Rome. He sent the man's head to the city and ordered that it be displayed. When he reported his victory in dispatches, he added a note stating that he had sent Albinus' head to be put on public view so that the people might know the extent of his anger against them. After settling affairs in Britain, he divided this region into two provinces, each under its own governor.[2] When he had also arranged matters in Gaul in what he considered the most advantageous way, he put all the friends of Albinus to death and confiscated their property, indifferent to whether they had supported the man by choice or by necessity. He then took his entire army to Rome in order to inspire the utmost terror there. When he had completed the journey at his usual rapid pace, he entered Rome, raging at Albinus' surviving friends. The citizens, carrying laurel branches, welcomed him with all honor and praise; the senate also came out to greet him, most of them standing before him in abject dread, convinced that he

---

[2] The army of Britain—three legions—was too large to be entrusted safely to the command of one governor. It was Severus' general policy to allow no governor of a province more than two legions.

BOOK THREE

would not spare their lives. Since his malevolence, a natural character trait, was deadly even when he had little provocation, now that he seemed to have every reason to treat them harshly, the members of the senate were terror-stricken.

4 After visiting the temple of Jupiter and offering sacrifices in the rest of the shrines, Severus entered the imperial palace. In honor of all his victories he made generous gifts to the people; distributing large sums of money to the soldiers, he granted them many privileges which they had not previ-
5 ously enjoyed. He was the first emperor to increase their food rations, to allow them to wear gold finger rings, and to permit them to live with their wives; these were indulgences hitherto considered harmful to military discipline and the proper conduct of war. Severus was also the first emperor to make a change in the harsh and healthy diet of the soldiers and to undermine their resolution in the face of severe hardships; moreover, he weakened their strict discipline and respect for their superiors by teaching them to covet money and by introducing them to luxurious living.

6 Having arranged these matters in the way he thought best, Severus went into the senate house and, mounting the imperial throne, launched a bitter attack upon the friends of Albinus, producing secret letters of theirs which he had found among the man's private correspondence. He blamed some for the extravagant gifts they had sent to Albinus, and brought other charges against the rest, complaining about the friendship of the men of the East for Niger and the sup-
7 port of the men of the West for Albinus. Then, without warning, he put to death all the eminent senators of that day, together with those men in the provinces who were noted for ancestry or wealth, pretending that he was avenging himself upon his enemies, when the truth was that he was driven by an insatiable lust for money; no other emperor was ever
8 so greedy for gold. Although in his steadfastness of purpose,

SEPTIMIUS SEVERUS

his endurance of toil, and his management of military affairs he was inferior to none of the respected emperors, still his love of money acquired unjustly and from murder done without provocation became an obsession with the man. His subjects submitted from fear rather than affection. He did try, however, to do what would please the people; he staged costly spectacles of every kind, killing on numerous occasions hundreds of animals of every species collected from all parts of the empire and from foreign lands as well, in connection with which he distributed lavish gifts. He held triumphal games for which he summoned dramatic actors and skilled athletes from every quarter. In his reign we saw every kind of show exhibited in all the theaters simultaneously, as well as night-long revels celebrated in imitation of the Mysteries.[3] The people of that day called them the Secular Games when they learned that they would be held only once every hundred years. Heralds were sent throughout Rome and Italy bidding all to come and see what they had never seen before and would never see again. It was thus made clear that the amount of time which elapsed between one celebration of the Secular Games and the next far exceeded the total span of any man's life.[4]

CHAPTER IX

SEVERUS now remained in Rome for a long time, during which his sons were partners with him in governing the empire. He was then seized with a desire to win glory for victories not only over fellow countrymen and Roman armies but also barbarians; using as an excuse for his action the friendship shown to Niger by Barsemius, king of the

---

[3] The Eleusinian Mysteries are the most famous of these orgiastic rites celebrated in secret in honor of Demeter and Dionysus.

[4] The *saeculum*, the longest span of human life, was fixed for the games of Severus in 204 as one hundred ten years.

BOOK THREE

2 Atrenians, he led his army off to the East. When he arrived there his intention was to invade Armenia also. But the king of the Armenians forestalled him by sending money, gifts, and hostages to support his plea for peace and by promising pacts and good will. After affairs in Armenia had thus turned out to his satisfaction, Severus marched against the Atrenian kingdom. At this time Abgarus, the Osroenian king, fled to Severus and gave him his children as a guaranty of his support; he also brought a great number of archers to fight in the Roman army.

3 After passing through the region between the Tigris and Euphrates rivers and the country of the Adiabenes, Severus hurried on into Arabia Felix, the country which produces the fragrant plants we use in our perfumes and incense. When he had destroyed many towns and villages there and had plundered the countryside, he came into the territory of the Atrenians, where he encamped and laid siege to the city of
4 Hatra. This city, located on top of a lofty mountain, was surrounded by a high, strong wall manned by many bowmen. After making camp, Severus' soldiers pressed the siege with all the power at their command, endeavoring to capture the city. Engines of every type were brought up to the wall,
5 and all the known tactics were tried. The Atrenians fought back bravely; pouring down a steady stream of stones and arrows, they did considerable damage to the army of Severus. Making clay pots, they filled them with winged insects, little poisonous flying creatures. When these were hurled down on the besiegers, the insects fell into the Romans' eyes and on all the unprotected parts of their bodies; digging in before they
6 were noticed, they bit and stung the soldiers. The Romans found the air at Hatra intolerable, stifling from the hot sun; they fell sick and died, and more casualties resulted from disease than from enemy action.
7 When the army, for the reasons mentioned above, had

SEPTIMIUS SEVERUS

abandoned all hope and the siege was at a stalemate, with the Romans losing instead of gaining ground, Severus led his troops away unsuccessful, fearing that he would lose his entire army.[5] The soldiers were unhappy that the siege had not turned out as successfully as they wished; accustomed to victory in all their battles, they believed that failure to win was actually defeat. But Fortune, by furthering his affairs at this time, provided Severus a measure of consolation; he did not return home without some success, and the truth is that he accomplished more than he had expected. The army, sailing in a large number of ships, was not borne to its intended destination on Roman-held shores, but after the current had carried the fleet a great distance, the legions disembarked on Parthian beaches at a spot within a few days' march of the road leading to Ctesiphon, where the royal palace of the Parthians was located. There the king was spending his time peacefully, thinking that the battles between Severus and the Atrenians were no concern of his. But the troops of the emperor, brought by the current to these shores against their will, landed and plundered the region, driving off for food all the cattle they found and burning all the villages as they passed. After proceeding a short distance, they stood at the gates of Ctesiphon, the capital city of the great king Artabanus. The Romans fell upon the unsuspecting barbarians, killing all who opposed them. Taking captive the women and children, they looted the entire city. After the king fled with a few horsemen, the Romans plundered the treasuries, seized the ornaments and jewels, and marched off.

Thus, more by luck than good judgment, Severus won the glory of a Parthian victory. And since these affairs turned out more successfully than he had any reason to hope, he sent dispatches to the senate and the people, extolling his exploits, and he had paintings of his battles and victories

---
[5] Hatra also successfully withstood a siege by Trajan. Cf. Dio 75.31.1-4.

BOOK THREE

put on public display. The senate voted him the titles formed from the names of the conquered nations, as well as all the rest of the usual honors.

CHAPTER X

WHEN he had settled affairs in the East, Severus returned to Rome, bringing with him his sons, who were then about eighteen years of age. On the journey he handled provincial problems as each situation demanded, and paid a visit to the troops in Moesia and Pannonia. His trip completed, he was welcomed as "Conqueror" by the Roman 2 people with extravagant praise and adoration. He then staged wild-animal shows for the people and celebrated, with merrymaking, holidays, festivals, and spectacles. After distributing lavish gifts and observing the customary festivities associated with a triumph, Severus remained in Rome for a number of years, presiding regularly in the courts, attending to civil matters, seeing to his sons' education, and keeping the 3 youths under control. But the lads (for they were already young men) were corrupted by the luxury and vice in Rome and by their boundless enthusiasm for shows, dancing, and chariot-driving. The two brothers were contentious from the beginning; as children they had been rivals over quail fights and cockfights, and had had the usual childish quar- 4 rels. Now their passion for shows and concerts made them constant competitors. Their followers and companions kept them at odds by fawning upon them and urging them to compete in enjoying youthful pleasures. When he was informed of this, Severus tried to reconcile his sons and keep them in hand.

5   Before his admission to the imperial ruling company, the elder son had the name Bassianus, but when he had the good fortune to receive the honor of a share in the imperial power,

SEPTIMIUS SEVERUS

Severus called the youth Antoninus,[6] wishing him to bear the name of Marcus. He also gave him a wife in the hope that marriage would mature him somewhat; the girl was the daughter of Plautianus, the praetorian prefect. As a youth this Plautianus had been a poor man (some say he was banished after being convicted of treason and many other crimes), but he was a fellow countryman of the emperor (Severus was also from Libya) and, as some say, he was related to the emperor; there are those too who charge him with being something worse, saying that when he was in the prime of youth he was the emperor's beloved. Consequently, Severus raised the man from a position of small and negligible honor to a post of great authority; by giving him the property of condemned men, he made Plautianus enormously wealthy. The emperor in fact shared the rule with no one except this man. Taking advantage of his authority, Plautianus left no act of violence undone and thus became more feared than any of the prefects before him. Severus united the two families by the marriage of his son to the daughter of Plautianus.

But Caracalla took no pleasure at all in this union, since he had married by compulsion, not by choice. He was exceedingly hostile to the girl, and to her father too, and refused to sleep or even eat with his wife; the truth is that he loathed her and daily promised to kill her and her father as soon as he became sole ruler of the empire. She reported these threats to her father and aroused his fury by stories of her husband's rancor.

---

[6] I have regularly substituted the more familiar "Caracalla" for Herodian's "Antoninus."

CHAPTER XI

OBSERVING that Severus was now old and constantly racked by disease, while Caracalla was a rash and reckless youth, Plautianus, in fear of these threats, elected to act first rather than to delay and suffer at his son-in-law's hands. Moreover, a number of things encouraged him to aspire to control of the empire: more money than anyone had ever seen before, his own personal army,[7] honors from the emperor, and his public attire. He wore the toga with the purple border and held rank equal to that of men who had twice served as consul; also he wore a sword. The prefect was the only official whose appearance suggested his importance. He was an object of dread when he appeared in public; not only did no one approach him, but even those who came upon him by chance turned aside to avoid him. The guards who preceded him did not allow anyone to stand near or to stare at him; all were ordered to step aside and keep their eyes fixed on the ground.

Severus was far from pleased when these matters were brought to his attention; he now became stern and harsh with Plautianus and tried to curb his excessive ostentation by depriving him of some of his authority. Plautianus refused to tolerate this reduction of power; bold enough to plot for the empire, he devised the following plan. In the Praetorian Guard was a tribune named Saturninus. This officer was devoted to the prefect; in fact, all his officers were devoted to Plautianus, but he had won the favor of the tribune by treating him with greater affection. Believing that Saturninus was the most trustworthy of the praetorian officers and the only one capable of using discretion and of carrying out secret orders, Plautianus summoned the man to him one eve-

---
[7] The Praetorian Guard.

ning after the rest had gone to bed. "Now you have an opportunity," he said, "to bring to a proper climax the good will and devotion you have always shown me, and I equally have an opportunity to repay you as you deserve and do you a comparable favor in return. The choice is yours either to become what you now see me to be and to secure this office of authority by succeeding me, or to die here and now, paying the penalty for disobedience. Do not by any means be overawed by the enormity of the deed I propose, and do not be disturbed by the title of emperor. You are the only one who can go into the room where the emperor and his son are sleeping, since you are in charge of the regular rounds of the night unit of the guard. Whatever you intend to do, you will do secretly and without interference; do not wait for me to issue the orders before you obey them. Go immediately to the imperial palace and, pretending to be carrying secret orders from me, go in and kill them. Show your courage by dispatching with ease an old man and a mere boy. And for sharing the risk and the danger, you will also share the highest honors when the deed is successfully done."

The tribune was astounded and perplexed by this proposal, but he was a man accustomed to keeping his wits about him (he was a Syrian, and the men from the East are rather more cunning in their thinking); observing the fury which gripped his commanding officer and well aware of his power, he did not oppose him, not wishing to be killed over these matters. Pretending therefore to be hearing things long prayed for and warmly welcomed, the tribune prostrated himself before Plautianus as if he were already emperor and begged him for a written memorandum ordering the murder. If a man were condemned to death without a trial, the tyrants customarily put the order in writing so that the sentence might not be carried out solely on verbal authority. Blinded by his ambition, Plautianus gave the tribune a directive in

BOOK THREE

writing and sent him off to commit the murders. He further ordered Saturninus, after killing the emperor and his son, to summon him, before the deed became known, that he might be in the palace before anyone realized that he was seizing the empire.

CHAPTER XII

AGREEING to those proposals, the tribune made his customary rounds through the entire imperial palace without interference. But knowing that it would be impossible for him to kill two emperors, especially since they were housed in different parts of the palace, Saturninus stood outside the bedroom of Severus and, summoning the imperial household guards, demanded to be taken to the emperor so that he might give him information involving his safety. The guards reported the matter to Severus and were ordered to bring the tribune before him. The tribune approached the emperor and said: "I have come to you, Master, as the man who sent me well knows, to be your assassin and murderer, but I hope and pray that I will be instead your benefactor and savior. Plautianus, scheming to seize the empire, ordered me to murder you and your son, and he issued this order not in words alone but in writing. This memorandum is my witness. I undertook the assignment because I was afraid that if I refused it he would entrust the task to someone else, and I have come here to disclose these matters to you so that his intrigues may not remain undetected." But even though Saturninus made these charges with much weeping, Severus was not immediately convinced. On the contrary, since he had great affection for the prefect, he suspected that the affair was a trick of some sort to deceive him; he believed that his son, in his hatred of the prefect and his daughter, had contrived a slanderous and fatal plot against the man. The emperor therefore sent for his son and reprimanded him for having devised such a scheme against a man kindly disposed toward the emperor and his intimate friend as well. At first Caracalla swore on his honor that he knew nothing about what the tribune was saying; but when the man insisted and produced the memorandum, the young emperor encouraged him, urging him to prove the truth of his charges. Realizing his danger and fearing the emperor's affection for Plautianus, the tribune now knew that if the plot remained confused and unproved, he could expect a death that would not be accidental. "Master," he said, "do you wish stronger proof or clearer evidence of some sort? Then allow me to go to the front of the palace and reveal to one of the men loyal to me that the murder is done. Trusting me, Plautianus will come here in the belief that he is occupying the deserted palace. When he arrives, it will be your task to discover the truth. Order complete silence about the palace so that the plan may not be upset by being previously discovered."

After making this proposal, the tribune ordered one of his most trusted men to carry a message to the prefect telling him to come to the palace as quickly as possible. The messenger was to say that both emperors were dead, and it was imperative that the prefect be inside the palace before the news was reported to the people. Then, with the Palatine Hill in his hands and the succession already settled, all the Romans, willingly or unwillingly, would offer allegiance not to an emperor to be chosen but to one already established. Believing this message, and with high hopes, Plautianus, though it was late at night, put on a breastplate beneath his robe for protection, mounted a chariot, and drove to the palace at top speed, accompanied by a few friends who were with him when the messenger came and who thought that he had received an emergency summons from the emperors. Plau-

BOOK THREE

9 tianus entered the palace unchallenged, since the guards were unaware of what was taking place. The tribune came forward to meet the prefect and set a trap for him: saluting Plautianus as emperor and taking him by the hand in the customary fashion under the circumstances, Saturninus led him into the bedroom where he said the bodies of the emperors had been thrown. Severus had already alerted some of the younger bodyguards to seize the prefect as he entered the room. Then Plautianus, who had expected a far different reception, was caught and held fast. When he saw both emperors standing before him, he was terror-stricken, and pleaded with them, trying to defend himself and swearing that it was all a mistake, a plot, a conspiracy against him.

10 When Severus reproached him with the many favors he had done him and the many honors he had awarded him, and Plautianus in his turn reminded the emperor of his previous loyalty and good will, Severus was beginning to believe the prefect until his robe fell open and revealed the breastplate beneath it. When he saw the armor, Caracalla, who was bold and quick to act and naturally hated the man, spoke up:

11 "How would you explain these two facts? First, that you came unordered to your emperors at night, and second, that you came here wearing that breastplate? Who goes to a feast or a revel in full armor?" After saying this, Caracalla ordered the tribune and the other praetorians present to draw

12 their swords and kill this proven enemy. Obeying without delay the young emperor's orders, they killed Plautianus and threw his body into the street, so that the affair might be clear to all and he would be vilified by those who despised him.

Such was the fate of Plautianus, who, maddened by his greed to have everything, was betrayed in the end by a faithless subordinate.

CHAPTER XIII

AFTER this time, Severus appointed two praetorian prefects. The emperor passed most of the remainder of his life on the imperial estates near the city and along the coast of Campania, presiding in the courts and attending to imperial affairs. He wished to keep his sons away from the luxury at Rome and wanted them to have the benefits of a wholesome life, especially when he observed that they were taking far more interest in shows than was proper for those of imperial rank. Because of their enthusiasm for these pastimes and the rivalry which kept them at odds and openly hostile, the brothers were in a constant state of turmoil, strife, and enmity. Caracalla became especially intolerable after he had removed Plautianus. Respect for his father and fear of him kept the youth from taking drastic action, but he plotted death in every form for his wife, Plautianus' daughter. Severus, however, sent the girl and her brother to Sicily, providing them with sufficient funds to live in comfort there. In doing this he was following the example of Augustus, who treated Antony's children in this way even though Antony was his enemy. Severus tried constantly to reconcile his sons and persuade them to live in peace and harmony. He kept reminding them of tales and plays of old, telling them time and again of the misfortunes suffered by royal brothers as a result of dissension. He showed them the treasuries and temples, overflowing with riches; he made it clear that they would never have to scheme abroad for money and power; resources at home were so plentiful that they could pay the soldiers with lavish generosity. The garrison at Rome had been quadrupled,[8] and the army encamped be-

---

[8] Almost surely an exaggeration. Severus did not increase the number of praetorian cohorts and added only one urban cohort.

BOOK THREE

fore the city was so powerful that there remained no foreign army strong enough to rival it in number of troops, in physical prowess, or in the amount of money available for pay. He told them, however, that all these were of no advantage to them as long as they remained hostile to each other and friction continued between them. By saying such things at every opportunity, now pleading, now rebuking, Severus tried to keep his sons under control and bring them into agreement. But the youths paid absolutely no attention to him; they rebelled and spent their time in pursuits even more reprehensible. Since they were vigorous youths and their imperial authority gave them an insatiable appetite for pleasures, each had his own group of loyal followers; these not only gratified the youths' desires and their enthusiasm for disgraceful practices, but they also constantly found new vices to bring pleasure to their favorite and chagrin to his brother. But Severus punished these parasites whenever he caught them performing such services.

CHAPTER XIV

IN THE midst of the emperor's distress at the kind of life his sons were leading and their disgraceful obsession with shows, the governor of Britain informed Severus by dispatches that the barbarians there were in revolt and overrunning the country, looting and destroying virtually everything on the island. He told Severus that he needed either a stronger army for the defense of the province or the presence of the emperor himself. Severus was delighted with this news: glory-loving by nature, he wished to win victories over the Britons to add to the victories and titles of honor he had won in the East and the West. But he wished even more to take his sons away from Rome so that they might settle down in the soldier's life under military discipline, far from the lux-

SEPTIMIUS SEVERUS

uries and pleasures in Rome. And so, although he was now well advanced in years and crippled with arthritis, Severus announced his expedition to Britain, and in his heart he was more enthusiastic than any youth. During the greater part of the journey he was carried in a litter, but he never remained very long in one place and never stopped to rest. He arrived with his sons at the coast sooner than anyone anticipated, outstripping the news of his approach. He crossed the channel and landed in Britain; levying soldiers from all these areas, he raised a powerful army and made preparations for the campaign.

Disconcerted by the emperor's sudden arrival, and realizing that this huge army had been assembled to make war upon them, the Britons sent envoys to Severus to discuss terms of peace, anxious to make amends for their previous errors. Seeking to prolong the war so as to avoid a quick return to Rome, and still wishing to gain a victory over the Britons and the title of honor too, Severus dismissed the envoys, refusing their offers, and continued his preparations for the war. He especially saw to it that dikes were provided in the marshy regions so that the soldiers might advance safely by running on these earth causeways and fight on a firm, solid footing. Most of the regions of Britain are marshy, since they are flooded continually by the tides of the ocean; the barbarians are accustomed to swimming or wading through these waist-deep marsh pools; since they go about naked, they are unconcerned about muddying their bodies. Strangers to clothing, the Britons wear ornaments of iron at their waists and throats; considering iron a symbol of wealth, they value this metal as other barbarians value gold. They tattoo their bodies with colored designs and drawings of all kinds of animals; for this reason they do not wear clothes, which would conceal the decorations on their bodies. Extremely savage and warlike, they are armed only with a spear and a

BOOK THREE

narrow shield, plus a sword that hangs suspended by a belt from their otherwise naked bodies. They do not use breastplates or helmets, considering them encumbrances in crossing the marshes. For all these reasons, Severus prepared whatever he thought would be of advantage to the Roman army and whatever would harass the barbarians and hamper their attacks.

9 When it seemed to him that all was in readiness for the campaign, Severus left the younger of his two sons, Geta, in the section of the province under Roman control; he instructed him to administer justice and attend to imperial affairs, leaving with him as advisers his more elderly friends. Then, accompanied by Caracalla, the emperor marched out
10 against the barbarians. After the troops had crossed the rivers and the earthworks which marked the boundary of the Roman empire in this region,[9] frequent battles and skirmishes occurred, and in these the Romans were victorious. But it was easy for the Britons to slip away; putting their knowledge of the surrounding area to good use, they disappeared in the woods and marshes. The Romans' unfamiliarity with the terrain prolonged the war.

CHAPTER XV

NOW a more serious illness attacked the aged emperor and forced him to remain in his quarters; he undertook, however, to send his son out to direct the campaign. Caracalla, however, paid little attention to the war, but rather attempted to gain control of the army. Trying to persuade the soldiers to look to him alone for orders, he courted sole rule in every possible way, including slanderous attacks upon
2 his brother. Considering his father, who had been ill for a

---
[9] The turf wall from the Firth of Forth to the Firth of Clyde built by Antoninus Pius in 142.

SEPTIMIUS SEVERUS

long time and slow to die, a burdensome nuisance, he tried to persuade the physicians to harm the old man in their treatments so that he would be rid of him more quickly. After a short time, however, Severus died, succumbing chiefly to grief, after having achieved greater glory in military affairs than any of the emperors who had preceded him. No emperor before Severus won such outstanding victories either in civil wars against political rivals or in foreign wars against barbarians. Thus Severus died [A.D. 211] after ruling for eighteen years, and was succeeded by his young sons, to whom he left an invincible army and more money than any emperor had ever left to his successors.

After his father's death, Caracalla seized control and immediately began to murder everyone in the court; he killed the physicians who had refused to obey his orders to hasten the old man's death and also murdered those men who had reared his brother and himself because they persisted in urging him to live at peace with Geta. He did not spare any of the men who had attended his father or were held in esteem by him. He undertook secretly to bribe the troop commanders by gifts and lavish promises, to induce them to persuade the army to accept him as sole emperor, and he tried every trick he knew against his brother. He failed to win the backing of the soldiers, however, for they remembered Severus and knew that the youths had been one and the same to him, and had been reared as equals from childhood; consequently they gave each brother the same support and loyalty. When the soldiers refused to uphold him, Caracalla signed a treaty with the barbarians, offering them peace and accepting their pledges of good faith. And now he abandoned this alien land and returned to his brother and mother. When the boys were together again, their mother tried to reconcile them, as did also men of repute and the friends of Severus who were their advisers. Since all these opposed his wishes, Caracalla,

BOOK THREE

from necessity, not from choice, agreed to live with Geta in peace and friendship, but this was pretended, not sincere. Thus, with both of them managing imperial affairs with equal authority, the two youths prepared to sail from Britain and take their father's remains to Rome. After burning his body and putting the ashes, together with perfumes, into an alabaster urn, they accompanied this urn to Rome and placed

8 it in the sacred mausoleum of the emperors.[10] They now crossed the channel with the army and landed as conquerors on the opposite shore of Gaul.

How Severus came to the end of his life and how his sons succeeded him in the imperial power, I have described in this book.

---
[10] The tomb of Hadrian beside the Tiber River.

BOOK FOUR

CARACALLA

CHAPTER I

THE activities of Severus during his eighteen years as emperor I have recounted in the preceding book. His sons, who were now young men, quarreled continually on the return journey to Rome with their mother. They did not use the same lodgings or even dine together, since they were extremely suspicious of all they ate and drank; each feared that the other would secretly get prior access to the kitchens and bribe the servants to use poison. This fear led the youths to complete the journey with even greater haste; for they believed that they would be safer in Rome where, by dividing the palace between them, each could manage his own affairs as he pleased in the most spacious dwelling in the entire city.

When they arrived in Rome, the people welcomed them with laurel branches and the senate, too, came out to greet them. The two youths headed the procession, wearing the imperial purple; the consuls for that year followed, carrying the urn which held the ashes of Severus. Then those who had come out to greet the young emperors passed by the urn

BOOK FOUR

4 and paid their respects to the emperor. The procession escorted the urn to the mausoleum where the remains of Marcus and his imperial predecessors are to be seen. After performing the rites prescribed for new emperors, the youths
5 entered the imperial palace. Each brother now took up residence in his half of the palace. Barricading the inner doors, they used in common only the public outer doors. Caracalla and Geta stationed their own private guards and were never seen together except briefly during their infrequent public appearances. But before doing anything else, the emperors performed the funeral rites for their father.

CHAPTER II

IT IS the Roman custom to elevate to divine status those emperors who at their death leave sons or designated successors; they call this honor deification. To begin with, public mourning, a combination of festive feeling and religious
2 ceremony, is observed throughout the entire city. After a costly funeral, the body of the emperor is interred in the customary fashion. But then a wax image is fashioned in the exact likeness of the corpse and placed on a large, high couch of ivory draped with coverings embroidered with gold. This wax figure lies on the couch like a sick man, pale and wan.
3 During most of the day people sit on each side of the couch; on the left is the entire senate, clad in black; on the right are all the women who, because of their husbands' or their fathers' positions, are entitled to honor and respect. None of these women wear gold ornaments or necklaces; each affects
4 the plain white garments associated with mourning. The various ceremonies mentioned above continue for seven days. Every day the physicians come and visit the couch; after pretending to examine the sick man, they announce daily that his condition is growing steadily worse. When it ap-

CARACALLA

pears that he is dead, the noblest of the Equestrians and picked young senators lift the couch and carry it along the Sacred Way to the Old Forum,[1] where the Roman magistrates give up their authority. Tiers of seats are erected on each side of the couch: on one side sits a chorus of children from the noblest and most distinguished families; on the other, a chorus of women who seem to deserve respect. In honor of the dead man each choral group sings hymns and paeans arranged in solemn and mournful measures. The couch is then carried out of the city to the Campus Martius, where, in the widest part of the plain, a square building has been constructed entirely of huge wooden beams in the shape of a house. The whole interior of this building is filled with firewood; and on the outside it is decorated with gold-embroidered hangings, ivory figures, colored paintings. Upon this structure rests a smaller second story, similar in shape and decoration, with open windows and doors. And there is a third and a fourth story, each smaller than the one beneath it; finally, the smallest story of all tops this structure. The building may be compared in shape to the lighthouses along the coast which by the light of their fires bring to safety ships in distress at night. The common name for such a lighthouse is Pharos.[2] They bring the couch to this structure and carry it up to the second story; then they add every kind of perfume and incense the earth provides, together with all the fruits, herbs, and juices that are gathered for their fragrance. Every province, every city, every man of fame and distinction is happy to furnish these last gifts in the emperor's honor. After a huge pile of aromatic material is collected, and the structure is completely filled, a cavalry exhibition is staged around the building; the entire Equestrian cavalry circles around it, following a fixed

---
[1] "Old" Forum, in contrast to the several imperial *Fora*.
[2] After the famous third-century B.C. Pharos at Alexandria.

BOOK FOUR

rotating pattern in the Pyrrhic choruses and maneuvers.[a] Chariots, too, are driven around the building in similar formations by drivers in purple robes; these chariots carry statues whose faces are those of Romans who fought or ruled in distinguished fashion. When these rites have been completed, the emperor's successor puts a torch to the structure, after which the people set it on fire on all sides. The flames easily and quickly consume the enormous pile of firewood and fragrant stuffs. From the topmost and smallest story, as if from a battlement, an eagle flies forth, soaring with the flames into the sky; the Romans believe that this eagle carries the soul of the emperor from the earth up to heaven. Thereafter the emperor is worshiped with the rest of the gods.

CHAPTER III

AFTER completing this ceremony of deification for their father, the youths returned to the palace. Open hostility followed, as they nurtured their hatred and hatched their plots. Each did everything in his power to eliminate his brother and secure the empire for himself alone. The honored and respected men of the city held divided opinions. Each of the youths privately solicited their support in secret letters, trying to win them by lavish promises. The majority favored Geta, who showed some evidence of a reasonable disposition, since he conducted himself mildly and moderately toward those who visited him, and devoted his time to the more serious pursuits. He studied with men respected for their learning and exercised frequently at the wrestling schools and the various gymnasia. Because he was kind and courteous to his associates and had an excellent reputation

---

[a] The Pyrrhic dance, with an origin in Greek myth, originated as a dance preparatory for war. Introduced into Rome by Julius Caesar, it was frequently performed thereafter.

and good name, he won the friendship and good will of most of the Romans. By contrast, Caracalla was harsh and savage in everything he did, scorning the pursuits mentioned above, and pretending a devotion to the military and martial life. Since he did everything in anger and used threats instead of persuasion, his friends were bound to him by fear, not by affection.

As the brothers were now completely at odds in even the most trivial matters, their mother undertook to effect a reconciliation. And at that time they concluded that it was best to divide the empire, to avoid remaining in Rome and continuing their intrigues. Summoning the advisers appointed by their father, with their mother present too, they decided to partition the empire: Caracalla to have all Europe, and Geta all the lands lying opposite Europe, the region known as Asia. For, they said, the two continents were separated by the Propontic Gulf as if by divine foresight. It was agreed that Caracalla establish his headquarters at Byzantium, with Geta's at Chalcedon in Bithynia; the two stations, on opposite sides of the straits, would guard each empire and prevent any crossings at that point. They decided too that it was best that the European senators remain in Rome, and those from the Asiatic regions accompany Geta. For his capital city, Geta said that either Antioch or Alexandria would be suitable, since, in his opinion, neither city was much inferior in size to Rome. Of the Southern provinces, the lands of the Moroccans, the Numidians, and the adjacent Libyans were given to Caracalla, and the regions east of these peoples were allotted to Geta. While they were engaged in cleaving the empire, all the rest kept their eyes fixed on the ground, but Julia cried out: "Earth and sea, my children, you have found a way to divide, and, as you say, the Propontic Gulf separates the continents. But your mother, how would you parcel her? How am I, unhappy,

BOOK FOUR

wretched—how am I to be torn and ripped asunder for the pair of you? Kill me first, and after you have claimed your share, let each one perform the funeral rites for his portion. Thus would I, too, together with earth and sea, be partitioned between you." After saying this, amid tears and lamentations, Julia stretched out her hands and, clasping them both in her arms, tried to reconcile them. And with all pitying her, the meeting adjourned and the project was abandoned. Each youth returned to his half of the imperial palace.

CHAPTER IV

BUT the hatred and dissension between them continued to grow. If it became necessary to appoint a governor or a magistrate, each wished to select a friend for the post. If they sat as judges, they handed down dissenting opinions, often to the ruin of those on trial; for rivalry counted more than justice to these two. Even at the shows the brothers took opposite sides. They tried every sort of intrigue; each, for example, attempted to persuade the other's cooks and cup-bearers to administer some deadly poison. It was not easy for either one to succeed in these attempts, however: both were exceedingly careful and took many precautions. Finally, unable to endure the situation any longer and maddened by the desire for sole power, Caracalla decided to act and advance his cause by sword or slaughter or die in a manner befitting his birth. Since his plotting was unsuccessful, he thought he must try some desperate and dangerous scheme; [so he killed his brother in the arms of their mother, and by this act really killed them both],[4] his mother dying of grief and his brother from treachery.

Mortally wounded, Geta died, drenching his mother's

---

[4] A lacuna here: Dio (78.2.3) says that Caracalla bribed several centurions to kill Geta in his mother's arms.

breast with his blood. Having succeeded in the murder, Caracalla ran from the room and rushed throughout the palace, shouting that he had escaped grave danger and had barely managed to save his life. He ordered the soldiers who guard the imperial palace to protect him and escort him to the praetorian camp, where he could be safely guarded, saying that if he remained in the imperial palace he would be murdered. Unaware of what had happened inside, the soldiers believed him and ran with him as he dashed ahead at full speed. Consternation seized the people when they saw the emperor speeding on foot through the middle of the city in the early evening. Rushing into the camp and into the temple where the standards and decorations of the guard were worshiped, Caracalla threw himself on the ground; in the chapel, he gave thanks and offered sacrifices for his safety. When this was reported to the praetorians, some of whom were in the baths, while others were already asleep, they hurriedly assembled in amazement. When he appeared before them, Caracalla did not immediately reveal what had happened; instead, shouting that he had escaped the deadly plots of an enemy and rival, he identified his assailant as his brother. He cried out that he had with difficulty emerged victorious, after a severe struggle with his enemies; but when he and his brother had put everything at stake, Fortune had chosen him as sole emperor. His motive in thus distorting the facts was his desire to have them hear from him what had happened rather than from someone else. In gratitude for his deliverance and in return for the sole rule, he promised each soldier 2,500 denarii and increased their ration allowance by one-half. He ordered the praetorians to go immediately and take the money from the temple depositories and the treasuries. In a single day he recklessly distributed all the money which Severus had collected and hoarded from the calamities of others over a period of eighteen years. When they heard

BOOK FOUR

about this vast amount of money, although they were aware of what had actually occurred, the murder having been made common knowledge by fugitives from the palace, the praetorians at once proclaimed Caracalla emperor and called Geta enemy.

CHAPTER V

THE emperor spent that night in the temple in the praetorian camp; then, growing bold because he had won over the soldiers by gifts, he came from the senate house accompanied by the entire guard, which was more heavily armed that was customary for the imperial escort. After he had gone in and offered sacrifices, Caracalla mounted the
2 imperial throne and addressed the senators as follows: "I am not unaware that every murder of a kinsman, immediately the deed is known, is despised, and that the name 'kinsman-killer' arouses harsh censure as soon as it falls upon the ear. Pity follows for the victims, hatred for the victors. In such cases it appears that the victim is abused, the victor abusing.
3 But if one were to consider the deed with sober judgment and not with sympathy for the fallen, and if he were to evaluate the victor's motive and intent, he would find that sometimes it is both reasonable and necessary for the man about to suffer an injury to defend himself and not stand passively and submit. Censure for cowardice follows when a man succumbs to disaster, but the winner gains, together with his
4 safety, a reputation for courage. As to the rest, all the plots he laid against me, using deadly poisons and every kind of treachery, these you can discover by the use of torture. For this reason I issued orders for Geta's servants to be present here so that you may learn the truth. Several have already been examined, and the results of the examination are available. In his final act of treachery, Geta burst in upon me while

CARACALLA

I was with my mother, accompanied by swordsmen whom he had obtained for this attempt upon my life. But I grasped the situation with great shrewdness and presence of mind and defended myself against an enemy who no longer displayed the attitude or feelings of a brother. Now to defend oneself against plots is not merely proper; it is a standard practice. Indeed, Romulus, the founder of this city, refused to allow his brother to ridicule what he had done. And I pass over without comment Germanicus, brother of Tiberius; Britannicus, Nero's brother; and Titus, brother of Domitian. Even Marcus himself, who professed to love philosophy and excellence, would not tolerate the arrogance of Lucius, his brother-in-law, and by a plot removed him from the scene. So I too, when poisons were prepared for me and a sword hung over me, defended myself against my enemy, for this is the name which describes his actions. First of all, you must give thanks to the gods for having preserved at least one of your emperors for you; then you must lay aside your differences of opinion in thought and in attitude and lead your lives in security, looking to one emperor alone. Jupiter, as he is himself sole ruler of the gods, thus gives to one ruler sole charge of mankind." After making these statements at the top of his voice, in a towering rage, he glared balefully at his brother's friends and returned to the palace, leaving most of the senators pale and trembling.

CHAPTER VI

GETA'S friends and associates were immediately butchered, together with those who lived in his half of the imperial palace. All his attendants were put to death too; not a single one was spared because of his age, not even the infants. Their bodies, after first being dragged about and subjected to every form of indignity, were placed in carts and

BOOK FOUR

taken out of the city; there they were piled up and burned
or simply thrown in the ditch. No one who had the slightest
acquaintance with Geta was spared: athletes, charioteers, and
singers and dancers of every type were killed. Everything
that Geta kept around him to delight eye and ear was destroyed. Senators distinguished because of ancestry or wealth
were put to death as friends of Geta upon the slightest unsupported charge of an unidentified accuser. He killed Commodus' sister, then an old woman, who as the daughter of
Marcus had been treated with honor by all the emperors.
Caracalla offered as his reason for murdering her the fact
that she had wept with his mother over the death of Geta.
His wife, the daughter of Plautianus, who was then in Sicily;
his first cousin Severus, the son of Pertinax; the son of Lucilla,
Commodus' sister; in fact, anyone who belonged to the imperial family and any senator of distinguished ancestry, all
were cut down to the last one. Then, sending his assassins
to the provinces, he put to death the governors and procurators friendly to Geta. Each night saw the murder of men in
every walk of life. He burned Vestal Virgins alive because
they were unchaste. Finally, the emperor did something that
had never been done before; while he was watching a chariot
race, the crowd insulted the charioteer he favored. Believing
this to be a personal attack, Caracalla ordered the Praetorian
Guard to attack the crowd and lead off and kill those shouting insults at his driver. The praetorians, given authority to
use force and to rob, but no longer able to identify those who
had shouted so recklessly (it was impossible to find them
in so large a mob, since no one admitted his guilt), took out
those they managed to catch and either killed them or, after
taking whatever they had as ransom, spared their lives, but
reluctantly.

CHAPTER VII

AFTER committing such crimes as these, hounded by his conscience and finding life in Rome intolerable, the emperor decided to leave the city to see to matters in the garrison camps and visit the provinces. Leaving Italy, he journeyed to the banks of the Danube, where he concerned himself with the northern part of his empire; at the same time he exercised by driving in chariot races and by fighting at close quarters with wild animals of every kind. Only occasionally did he sit as judge, although he was quick to grasp the essentials of a case in court and quick to pass judgment on the basis of the arguments presented. He grew especially fond of the Germans in those regions; after gaining their friendship, he entered into alliances with them, and selected for his personal bodyguard the strongest and most handsome young men. He frequently put off the Roman cloak and donned German dress, appearing in the short, silver-embroidered cloaks which they customarily wear, augmented by a yellow wig with the locks arranged in the German style. Delighted with the emperor's antics, the barbarians became very fond of him, as did the Roman soldiers also, particularly because of his lavish gifts of money but also because he always played the soldier's part. If a ditch had to be dug anywhere, the emperor was the first man to dig; if it were necessary to bridge a stream or pile up a high rampart, it was the same; in every task involving labor of hand or body, the emperor was first man to the job. He set a frugal table and even went so far as to use wooden dishes at his meals. He ate the bread that was available; grinding with his own hands his personal ration of grain, he made a loaf, baked it in the ashes, and ate it. Scorning luxuries, he used whatever was cheapest and issued to the poorest soldier. He pretended to be delighted when they called him fellow soldier instead of emperor. For the most part he marched with the troops, carrying his own arms and rarely using a chariot or a horse. Occasionally he even placed the standards of the legions on his shoulders and bore them along; these standards, tall and decorated with many gold ornaments, were a heavy burden for even the strongest soldiers. For these actions Caracalla won the affection of the soldiers by his military prowess and gained their admiration by his feats of strength. And it is certainly true that the performance of such strenuous tasks by a man of small stature was worthy of admiration.

CHAPTER VIII

CARACALLA, after attending to matters in the garrison camps along the Danube River, went down into Thrace at the Macedonian border, and immediately he became Alexander the Great. To revive the memory of the Macedonian in every possible way, he ordered statues and paintings of his hero to be put on public display in all cities. He filled the Capitol, the rest of the temples, indeed, all Rome, with statues and paintings designed to suggest that he was a second Alexander. At times we saw ridiculous portraits, statues with one body which had on each side of a single head the faces of Alexander and the emperor. Caracalla himself went about in Macedonian dress, affecting especially the broad sun hat and short boots. He enrolled picked youths in a unit which he labeled his Macedonian phalanx; its officers bore the names of Alexander's generals. He also summoned picked young men from Sparta and formed a unit which he called his Laconian and Pitanate battalion.

After doing this, he arranged matters in the cities in that region to his satisfaction and then proceeded to Pergamum in Asia Minor, to try the healing treatments of Aesculapius.

CARACALLA

When he arrived in that city he made what use he wished of the dream treatments[5] and continued on to Troy. He visited all the ruins of that city, coming last to the tomb of Achilles; he adorned this tomb lavishly with garlands of flowers, and immediately he became Achilles. Casting about for a Patroclus, he found one ready to hand in Festus, his favorite freedman, keeper of the emperor's daily record book. This Festus died at Troy; some say he was poisoned so that he could be buried as Patroclus, but others say he died of disease. Caracalla ordered a huge pyre of logs to be erected and the body of Festus placed in the center. After sacrificing animals of all kinds, the emperor set fire to the funeral pile; then, taking a bowl and pouring a libation, he offered prayers to the winds. Since he was almost entirely bald, he made himself ridiculous when he wished to place his curls upon the blaze; he did, however, shear off what little hair he had.[6] Among generals, Caracalla admired the Roman Sulla and the Carthaginian Hannibal, and set up statues and paintings of these two.

The emperor then left Troy and traveled through the rest of Asia, Bithynia, and the remaining provinces. After tending to affairs in these regions, he came to Antioch. Given a warm welcome there, he remained for some time. While in the city he sent letters to Alexandria, pretending to be eager to visit the city founded by Alexander and to pay his respects to the god whom the Alexandrians worship above all other deities.[7] He pretended that the two compelling reasons for his proposed visit were the worship of the god and the memory of

---

[5] The healing ritual known as incubation, or temple sleep. After the preliminary ritual, the patient lay down to sleep in an open colonnade. During the night, Aesculapius appeared in a dream, gave treatment—even occasionally performed an operation—and the patient left the next morning, cured.

[6] Cf. *Iliad* 23.168–185.

[7] Serapis (Sarapis) was the chief god in the Egyptian cult of deities under the empire; as Serapis Polieus he was the chief god of Alexandria.

BOOK FOUR

his hero Alexander. He therefore ordered a number of hecatombs of cattle to be prepared, together with offerings of every kind. When these matters were reported to the people of Alexandria, who are by nature carefree and very easily aroused on the slightest provocation, they were overjoyed to learn of the emperor's enthusiastic interest and his great affection for them. They prepared a superlative reception for the emperor. Everywhere bands were performing on all kinds of musical instruments and playing a variety of melodies. Billows of perfume and the smoke of incense spread sweet aromas throughout the city. The emperor was honored with torchlight parades and showers of floral bouquets. When he entered the city, accompanied by his entire army, Caracalla went first into the temple,[8] where he sacrificed many hecatombs of cattle and heaped the altars with frankincense. Leaving the temple for the tomb of Alexander, he removed there his purple robe, his finger rings set with precious gems, together with his belts and anything else of value on his person, and placed them upon the tomb.

CHAPTER IX

WHEN they saw what the emperor was doing, the people rejoiced and celebrated, making merry the whole night long, but they did not know his secret intent. In all his actions Caracalla was playing the hypocrite; his true plan was to destroy most of them. The source of the enmity he was concealing was this. While he was still living in Rome, both during his brother's lifetime and after his murder, it was reported to him that the Alexandrians were making endless jokes about him. The people of that city are by nature fond of jesting at the expense of those in high places. However witty these clever remarks may seem to

---
[8] The magnificent Serapeum.

CARACALLA

those who make them, they are very painful to those who are ridiculed. Particularly galling are quips that reveal one's shortcomings. Thus they made many jokes at the emperor's expense about his murdering his brother, calling his aged mother Jocasta,[9] and mocking him because, in his insignificance, he imitated the bravest and greatest of heroes, Alexander and Achilles. But although they thought they were merely joking about these matters, in reality they were causing the naturally savage and quick-tempered Caracalla to plot their destruction.

The emperor therefore joined the Alexandrians in celebrating and merrymaking. When he observed that the city was overflowing with people who had come in from the surrounding area, he issued a public proclamation directing all the young men to assemble in a broad plain, saying that he wished to organize a phalanx in honor of Alexander similar to his Macedonian and Spartan battalions, this unit to bear the name of the hero. He ordered the youths to form in rows so that he might approach each one and determine whether his age, size of body, and state of health qualified him for military service. Believing him to be sincere, all the youths, quite reasonably hopeful because of the honor he had previously paid the city, assembled with their parents and brothers, who had come to celebrate the youths' expectations. Caracalla now approached them as they were drawn up in groups and passed among them, touching each youth and saying a word of praise to this one and that one until his entire army had surrounded them. The youths did not notice or suspect anything. After he had visited them all, he judged that they were now trapped in the net of steel formed by his soldiers' weapons, and left the field, accompanied by his personal bodyguard. At a given signal the soldiers fell upon the encircled youths, attacking them and any others present. They

---
[9] The mother and wife of Oedipus.

BOOK FOUR

cut them down, these armed soldiers fighting against unarmed, surrounded boys, butchering them in every conceivable fashion. Some did the killing while others outside the ring dug huge trenches; they dragged those who had fallen to these trenches and threw them in, filling the ditch with bodies. Piling on earth, they quickly raised a huge burial mound. Many were thrown in half-alive, and others were forced in unwounded. A number of soldiers perished there too; for all who were thrust into the trench alive, if they had the strength, clung to their killers and pulled them in with them. So great was the slaughter that the wide mouths of the Nile and the entire shore around the city were stained red by the streams of blood flowing through the plain. After these monstrous deeds, Caracalla left Alexandria and returned to Antioch.

CHAPTER X

NOT long after this, Caracalla, desirous of gaining the title "Parthicus" and of being able to report to the Romans that he had conquered all the Eastern barbarians, even though there was peace everywhere, devised the following plan. He wrote a letter to the king of Parthia (his name was Artabanus) and sent to him an embassy laden with gifts of expensive materials and fine workmanship. He wrote to the king that he wished to marry his daughter; that it was not fitting that he, emperor and son of an emperor, be the son-in-law of a lowly private citizen. His wish was to marry a princess, the daughter of a great king. He pointed out that the Roman and the Parthian empires were the largest in the world; if they were united by marriage, one empire without a rival would result when they were no longer divided by a river. The rest of the barbarian nations now not subject to their authority could easily be reduced, as they were governed by tribes and confederacies. Furthermore, the Roman infantry were invincible in close-quarter combat with spears, and the Parthians had a large force of highly skilled horse-archers. The two forces, he said, complemented each other; by waging war together, they could easily unite the entire inhabited world under a single crown. Since the Parthians produced spices and excellent textiles and the Romans metals and manufactured articles, these products would no longer be scarce and smuggled by merchants; rather, when there was one world under one supreme authority, both peoples would enjoy these goods and share them in common.

At first the Parthian king did not approve of the proposals in Caracalla's letters, saying that it was not proper for a barbarian to marry a Roman. What accord could there be when they did not understand each other's language and differed so radically in diet and dress? Surely, the king said, there are many distinguished Romans, one of whose daughters he could marry, just as for him there were the Arsacids;[10] it was not fitting that either race be bastardized.

CHAPTER XI

THE Parthian's initial replies were of this type, and he declined Caracalla's offer of an alliance. But when the emperor persisted and with many gifts and oaths swore to his enthusiasm for the marriage and his good will toward the Parthians, Artabanus was won over; addressing Caracalla as his future son-in-law, he promised him his daughter in marriage. When the news was made public, the barbarians prepared for the reception of the emperor of the Romans and rejoiced in the hope of permanent peace. Having crossed the rivers unopposed, Caracalla entered the barbarians' land as if it were already his. Sacrifices were offered to him every-

---

[10] The royal dynasty of Parthia.

BOOK FOUR

where; the altars were decked with wreaths, and perfumes and every kind of incense were scattered in his path. Caracalla pretended to be delighted by the barbarians' attentions and continued his advance. He had now completed the greater part of his journey and was approaching the palace of Artabanus. The king did not wait to receive the emperor but came out to meet him in the plain before the city, welcoming his son-in-law, the bridegroom of his daughter. All the Parthians, crowned with the traditional flowers and wearing robes embroidered in gold and various colors, celebrated the occasion, dancing wildly to the music of flutes and the throbbing of drums. They take delight in such orgiastic dancing, especially when they are drunk. Abandoning their horses and laying aside their quivers and bows, the whole populace came together to drink and pour libations. A huge mob of barbarians gathered and stood about casually, wherever they happened to be, eager to see the bridegroom and expecting nothing out of the ordinary. Then the signal was given, and Caracalla ordered his army to attack and massacre the spectators. Astounded by this onslaught, the barbarians turned and fled, wounded and bleeding. Artabanus himself, snatched up and placed on a horse by some of his personal bodyguards, barely escaped with a few companions. The rest of the Parthians, lacking their indispensable horses, were cut down (for they had sent the horses out to graze and were standing about). They were unable to escape by running, either; their long, loose robes, hanging to their feet, tripped them up. Naturally they did not have their quivers and bows with them; what need for weapons at a wedding? After slaughtering a great number of the enemy and taking much booty and many prisoners, Caracalla marched away from the city unopposed. En route he burned the towns and villages and permitted his soldiers to carry off as much as they could of anything they wanted.

CARACALLA

Such was the nature of the disaster which the barbarians suffered when they were not anticipating anything of the kind. After harassing most of the Parthian empire, Caracalla, since his troops were weary by now of looting and killing, went off to Mesopotamia. From there he sent word to the senate and the Roman people that the entire East was subdued and that all the kingdoms in that region had submitted to him. The senators were not unaware of what had actually happened (for it is impossible to conceal an emperor's acts); nevertheless, fear and the desire to flatter led them to vote the emperor all the triumphal honors. Thereafter, Caracalla spent some time in Mesopotamia, where he devoted himself to chariot-driving and to fighting all kinds of wild animals.

CHAPTER XII

CARACALLA had two generals in his army: Adventus, an old man, who had some skill in military matters but was a layman in other fields and unacquainted with civil administration; and Macrinus, experienced in public affairs and especially well trained in law. Caracalla often ridiculed Macrinus publicly, calling him a brave, self-styled warrior, and carrying his sarcasm to the point of shameful abuse. When the emperor learned that Macrinus was overfond of food and scorned the coarse, rough fare which Caracalla the soldier enjoyed, he accused the general of cowardice and effeminacy, and continually threatened to murder him. Unable to endure these insults any longer, the angry Macrinus grew dangerous.

This is the way the affair turned out; it was, at long last, time for Caracalla's life to come to an end. The emperor, always excessively curious, wished not only to know everything about the affairs of men but also to meddle in divine

BOOK FOUR

matters. Since he suspected everyone of plotting against him, he consulted all the oracles and summoned prophets, astrologers, and entrail-examiners from all over the world; no one who practiced the magic art of prophecy escaped him. But when he began to suspect that these men were not prophesying truthfully but were flattering him, Caracalla wrote a letter to Materianus, to whom he had entrusted control of affairs at Rome. This Materianus he considered the most trustworthy of his friends, the only one with whom he shared the imperial secrets. He ordered Materianus to locate all the most highly skilled prophets and to make use of their magic arts to discover whether anyone was plotting to seize the empire. Materianus obeyed the emperor's orders to the letter, and whether because the spirits actually revealed these things to him or because he was eager to remove Macrinus, he sent Caracalla a dispatch informing him that Macrinus was conspiring to seize control of the empire and must be eliminated. Sealing this letter, he gave it routinely with the other dispatches to the couriers, who did not, of course, know what they were carrying. Completing the journey with their usual speed, the messengers approached Caracalla after he had already donned his racing uniform and was about to climb into the waiting chariot, and gave him the whole bundle of dispatches, including the letter concerning Macrinus. Caracalla, about to drive off, and intent upon the coming race, ordered Macrinus, who was standing nearby alone, to examine the dispatches and, if they contained anything urgent, to inform him. If, however, there was nothing pressing in them, he was to handle them himself in the usual manner, in his capacity as praetorian prefect. The emperor frequently ordered Macrinus to do this. After giving these directions, Caracalla turned to his race. Macrinus withdrew and opened the dispatches in private; when he found the one containing his own death sentence, he saw clearly the danger which threat-

CARACALLA

ened him. Knowing the emperor's nature, and realizing that the death sentence contained in the letter would give the emperor legitimate cause for putting him to death, Macrinus removed this letter from the pile and reported that the rest were of the routine sort.

CHAPTER XIII

THE prefect, fearing that Materianus might send this information to the emperor a second time, decided to act now rather than wait and suffer the consequences. This is what he did. In Caracalla's bodyguard was a centurion named Martialis, who was always in the emperor's escort. A few days earlier, Caracalla had executed the centurion's brother on an unproved charge. Moreover, the emperor continually insulted the man, calling him cowardly, effeminate, and Macrinus' darling. Learning that Martialis was exceedingly grieved by his brother's death and could no longer endure the emperor's insults, Macrinus summoned the centurion (in whom he had confidence because the man had served him before, and had received many favors from him). The prefect persuaded Martialis to be on the watch for a suitable opportunity to carry out a plot against the emperor. Won over by Macrinus' promises, Martialis, since he hated the emperor and was eager to avenge his brother, gladly promised to do the deed when the proper occasion arose.

Not long after they made this agreement, it happened that Caracalla, who was spending the time at Carrhae in Mesopotamia, conceived a desire to leave the imperial quarters and visit the Temple of the Moon, for Selene is the goddess whom the natives particularly adore. The temple was located some distance from Carrhae, and the journey was a long one. Therefore, to avoid involving the entire army, Caracalla made the trip with a few horsemen, intending to sacrifice

BOOK FOUR

4 to the goddess and then return to the city. At the halfway point he stopped to relieve himself; ordering his escort to ride off, he went apart with a single attendant. All the horsemen turned aside and withdrew for some distance, respecting the
5 emperor's modesty. But when Martialis, who was looking for just such an opportunity, saw Caracalla alone, he ran toward him as if the emperor had summoned him by a gesture to question him or receive some information. Standing over Caracalla after he had uncovered himself, Martialis stabbed the emperor from behind with a dagger he had concealed in his hand. The blow under the shoulder was fatal, and Caracalla died, unsuspecting and undefended.[11] When
6 the emperor fell, Martialis leaped upon his horse and fled. Those favorites of Caracalla, the German cavalry who served as his bodyguard, were closer to the scene than the rest, and hence were the first to realize what had happened. These horsemen set out in pursuit of Martialis and cut him down.
7 When the rest of the army learned what had occurred, they hurried to the spot, and Macrinus was the first to arrive; standing over the body, he pretended to wail and lament for the emperor. The whole army was grieved and distressed by the affair; they felt they had lost a fellow soldier, a comrade-in-arms, rather than their emperor. And yet they never suspected that it was a plot of Macrinus; they believed that Martialis had done it because of his personal hatred for the
8 emperor. Then the soldiers retired, each to his own tent. After burning the body on a pyre and placing the ashes in an urn, Macrinus sent it for burial to the emperor's mother in Antioch. As a result of these similar disasters which befell her two sons, Julia died, either by her own hand or by the emperor's order. Such was the fate suffered by Caracalla and his mother Julia, who lived in the manner I have described above. Caracalla had served as emperor without his father and brother for eleven years.

[11] April 8, 217.

CHAPTER XIV

AFTER Caracalla's death, the bewildered soldiers were at a loss as to what to do. For two days they were without an emperor while they looked for someone to fill the office. And now it was reported that Artabanus was approaching with a huge army, seeking a legitimate revenge for the Parthians whom Caracalla had murdered under a truce and in time of peace. The army first chose Adventus as their emperor because he was a military man and a praetorian prefect of considerable ability; he declined the honor, however, pleading his advanced age. They then decided upon Macrinus, influenced by their tribunes, who were close friends of the general and were suspected of having been involved in the plot against Caracalla. Later, after Macrinus' death, these tribunes were punished, as we shall relate in the pages to follow. Macrinus thus received the office of emperor not so much because of the soldiers' affection and loyalty as from necessity and the urgency of the impending crisis.

While these events were taking place, Artabanus was marching toward the Romans with a huge army, including a strong cavalry contingent and a powerful unit of archers and those mail-clad soldiers who hurl spears from camels. When the approach of Artabanus was reported, Macrinus called the soldiers together and addressed them as follows: "That all of you regret the passing of such an emperor, or, more accurately, fellow soldier, is hardly surprising. But to endure misfortunes and disasters with equanimity is the part of intelligent men. Truly the memory of Caracalla is locked in our hearts, and to those who come after us will be handed down this memory, which will bring him everlasting fame for his great and noble deeds, his love and affection for you, and his labors and comradeship with you. But now it is time for us, since we have paid the last of the prescribed honors to the memory of the dead and have performed his funeral rites, to look to the present emergency. You see the barbarian with his whole Eastern horde already upon us, and Artabanus seems to have good reason for his enmity. We provoked him by breaking the treaty, and in a time of complete peace we started a war. Now the whole Roman empire depends upon our courage and loyalty. This is no quarrel about boundaries or river beds; everything is at stake in this dispute in which we face a mighty king fighting for his children and kinsmen who, he believes, have been murdered in violation of solemn oaths. Therefore let us take up our arms and our battle stations in the customary Roman good order. In the fighting, the undisciplined mob of barbarians, assembled only for temporary duty, may prove its own worst enemy. Our battle tactics and our stern discipline, together with our combat experience, will insure our safety and their destruction. Therefore, with hopes high, contest the issue as it is fitting and traditional for Romans to do. Thus will you repel the barbarians, and by winning a great and glorious reputation you will make it clear to the Romans and to all men—and you will likewise confirm that previous victory—that you did not deceive the barbarians by fraudulently and treacherously breaking your treaty with them, but that you conquered and won by force of arms."

After this speech the soldiers, recognizing the necessity of the matter, took up battle stations and remained under arms.

CHAPTER XV

ARTABANUS appeared at sunrise with his vast army. When they had saluted the sun, as was their custom, the barbarians, with a deafening cheer, charged the Roman line, firing their arrows and whipping on their horses. The Romans had arranged their divisions carefully to insure a stable front; the cavalry and the Moroccan javelin men were stationed on the wings, and the open spaces were filled with light-armed and mobile troops that could move rapidly from one place to another. And so the Romans received the charge of the Parthians and joined battle. The barbarians inflicted many wounds upon the Romans from above, and did considerable damage by the showers of arrows and the long spears of the mail-clad camel riders. But when the fighting came to close quarters, the Romans easily defeated the barbarians; for when the swarms of Parthian cavalry and hordes of camel riders were mauling them, the Romans pretended to retreat and then they threw down caltrops and other keen-pointed iron devices. Covered by the sand, these were invisible to the horsemen and the camel riders and were fatal to the animals. The horses, and particularly the tender-footed camels, stepped on these devices and, falling, threw their riders. As long as they are mounted on horses and camels, the barbarians in those regions fight bravely, but if they dismount or are thrown, they are very easily captured; they cannot stand up to hand-to-hand fighting. And, if they find it necessary to flee or pursue, the long robes which hang loosely about their feet trip them up.

On the first and second days the two armies fought from morning until evening, and when night put an end to the fighting, each side withdrew to its own camp, claiming the victory. On the third day they came again to the same field to do battle; then the barbarians, who were far superior in numbers, tried to surround and trap the Romans. The Romans, however, no longer arranged their divisions to obtain depth; instead, they broadened their front and blocked every attempt at encirclement. So great was the number of slaughtered men and animals that the entire plain was covered with the dead; bodies were piled up in huge mounds, and the camels especially fell in heaps. As a result, the soldiers were

BOOK FOUR

hampered in their attacks; they could not see each other for the high and impassable wall of bodies between them. Prevented by this barrier from making contact, each side withdrew to its own camp.

6   Macrinus knew that Artabanus was making so strong a stand and battling so fiercely only because he thought that he was fighting Caracalla; the barbarian always tires of battle
7   quickly and loses heart unless he is immediately victorious. But on this occasion the Parthians resolutely stood their ground and renewed the struggle after they had carried off their dead and buried them, for they were unaware that the cause of their hatred was dead. Macrinus therefore sent an embassy to the Parthian king with a letter telling him that the emperor who had wronged him by breaking his treaties and violating his oaths was dead and had paid a richly deserved penalty for his crimes. Now the Romans, to whom the empire really belonged, had entrusted to Macrinus the management of
8   their realm. He told Artabanus that he did not approve of Caracalla's actions and promised to restore all the money he had lost. Macrinus offered friendship to Artabanus instead of hostility and assured him that he would confirm peace between them by oaths and treaties. When he learned this and was informed by envoys of Caracalla's death, Artabanus believed that the treaty breaker had suffered a suitable punishment; as his own army was riddled with wounds, the king
9   signed a treaty of peace with Macrinus, content to recover the captives and stolen money without further bloodshed. The Parthian then returned to his own country, and Macrinus led his army out of Mesopotamia and hurried on to Antioch.

BOOK FIVE

MACRINUS, ELAGABALUS

CHAPTER I

CARACALLA'S life and death have been described in the preceding book. While at Antioch, Macrinus wrote a letter to the senate and the Roman people in which he said the following: "You are familiar with the course of my life from its very beginning. You know my inclination toward uprightness of character, and are aware of the moderation with which I previously managed affairs, when my power and authority were little inferior to that of the emperor himself. For that reason, and since the emperor sees fit to put his trust in the praetorian prefects, I do not think it necessary for me to address you at great length. You know that I did not approve of the emperor's actions. Indeed, I frequently risked my life on your behalf when he listened to random charges and attacked you without mercy. He criticized me harshly too, often publicly complaining about my moderation and my restraint in dealing with those under my authority, and ridiculing me for my easygoing ways and mild manner. He delighted in flatterers and men who encouraged him to cruelty and gave him good reason for his

BOOK FIVE

savagery by arousing his anger with slanderous charges. These people he considered his loyal friends. I, on the other hand, have from the beginning been mild, moderate, and agreeable. We brought the war against the Parthians to a conclusion, a critical struggle involving the safety of the whole Roman empire. In our courageous opposition to the Parthians we proved in no way inferior to them, and in signing a treaty of peace we made a loyal friend instead of a dangerous enemy of a great king, who had marched against us at the head of a formidable army. Under my rule all men shall live in peace, and senatorial rule shall replace the autocracy. But let no one think me unworthy of my post, and let no one believe that Fortune blundered in raising me to this position, even though I am of the Equestrian order.[1] For what advantage is there in nobility of birth unless it be combined with a beneficent and kindly nature? The gifts of Fortune fall upon the undeserving also, but it is the excellence of his own soul which brings every man his measure of personal glory. Nobility of birth, wealth, and the like are presumed to bring happiness, but, since they are bestowed by someone else, they deserve no praise. Virtue and kindness, on the other hand, besides commanding admiration, win a full measure of praise for anyone who succeeds by his own efforts. What, may I ask, did the noble birth of Commodus profit you? Or the fact that Caracalla inherited the throne from his father? Indeed, having received the empire as legal heirs, the two youths abused their high office and conducted themselves insolently, as if the empire were their own personal possession by right of inheritance. But those who receive the empire from your hands are eternally in your debt for the favor, and they undertake to repay those who have done them previous good services. The noble ancestry of the highborn emperors leads them to commit insolent acts out of con-

---
[1] Macrinus was the first emperor who was not of the senatorial order.

tempt for their subjects, whom they regard as far below them. By contrast, those who come to the throne as a result of temperate behavior treat the post with respect, since they secured it by toil; they continue to show to those who were formerly their superiors the same deference and esteem they were accustomed to show. I intend to have you senators as my associates and assistants in managing the empire, and I intend to do nothing without your approval. You shall live in freedom and security, enjoying the privileges of which you were deprived by your nobly born emperors and which Marcus, of old, and Pertinax, recently, undertook to restore to you; the latter also are emperors who came to the throne from private circumstances. Surely it is better for a man to provide his descendants with the glorious beginnings of a family line than, having inherited ancestral glory, to disgrace it by outrageous behavior."

CHAPTER II

AFTER they heard this message, the cheering senate voted Macrinus all the imperial honors. The fact is, however, that they rejoiced not so much at Macrinus' succession as at their own deliverance from Caracalla. Every man, but especially those who had any claim to merit or distinction, felt that he had escaped a sword suspended over his head. All informers and all slaves who had betrayed their masters were crucified; the city of Rome and virtually the entire Roman empire were purged of these scoundrels. Some were killed, others exiled; any who managed to escape, prudently laid low. As a result, men lived in complete security and in a semblance of freedom during the single year in which Macrinus was emperor. But he made a great mistake in not immediately disbanding the armies, sending the soldiers back to their regular stations, and hurrying off to a Rome eager to welcome him, where the people were shouting for him on every occasion. Instead, he loitered at Antioch, cultivating his beard. He moved with greater deliberation than was necessary, and to those who approached him he made replies that were very slow, difficult to understand, and often inaudible because of the softness of his voice. In doing all this he was imitating Marcus, but he failed to follow that emperor's example in other respects; he indulged in endless luxuries and devoted his time to dancing shows, recitals of every kind of music, and exhibitions of pantomime, while neglecting the administration of the empire. He appeared in public resplendent in brooches and wearing a stomacher lavishly adorned with gold and precious gems, extravagances of which the Roman soldiers did not approve because such ornaments seemed more appropriate to barbarians and women. The soldiers were not at all pleased by what they saw; they disapproved of his way of life as too dissolute for a military man. When they contrasted it with their recollection of Caracalla's daily routine, which, being soldierly and austere, was the exact opposite, they had only contempt for Macrinus' extravagant behavior. Other circumstances increased their irritation; still living in tents and sometimes short of supplies in a foreign land, even though a state of peace seemed to exist, they longed to return to their regular stations. When they saw Macrinus' luxury and laxity, they rebelled and spoke bitterly about him, praying for even a flimsy excuse to rid themselves of this annoyance.

CHAPTER III

THEREFORE it was inevitable that Macrinus, after ruling for a single year, should lose the empire and his life when Fortune provided the soldiers with a trivial and inadequate excuse for accomplishing their desire. Julia, wife

of Severus and mother of Caracalla, had a sister, Maesa, a
Phoenician named after the city of Emesa in that country.
During her sister's imperial career, the many years that
Severus and Caracalla were emperors, this woman lived in
the imperial palace. After the assassination of Caracalla and
Julia's death, Macrinus ordered Maesa to return to her own
estates in Phoenicia, allowing her to live there in full possession of her property. Since Maesa had lived for a long
time under imperial protection, she had amassed a huge personal fortune. Thus the old woman now went off to live on
her estates. Maesa had two daughters. The elder was called
Soaemias; the younger, Mamaea. Each of the girls had an
only son: Soaemias' son was named Bassianus; Mamaea's,
Alexianus. These boys, who were reared by their mothers
and their grandmother, were at that time about fourteen and
ten, respectively. They were priests of the sun god, whom
their countrymen worship under the Phoenician name Elagabalus.[2] A huge temple was erected to this god, lavishly
decorated with gold, silver, and costly gems. Not only is this
god worshiped by the natives, but all the neighboring rulers
and kings send generous and expensive gifts to him each
year. No statue made by man in the likeness of the god stands
in this temple, as in Greek and Roman temples. The temple
does, however, contain a huge black stone with a pointed end
and round base in the shape of a cone. The Phoenicians
solemnly maintain that this stone came down from Zeus;
pointing out certain small figures in relief, they assert that it
is an unwrought image of the sun, for naturally this is what
they wish to see. Bassianus was the chief priest of this god.
(Since he was the elder of the boys, the priesthood had been
entrusted to him.) He went about in barbarian dress, wearing
long-sleeved purple tunics embroidered with gold which
hung to his feet; robes similarly decorated with gold and

---

[2] The Baal of Emesa. The spelling of "Elagabalus" varies.

BOOK FIVE

7 purple covered his legs from hip to toe, and he wore a crown of varicolored precious gems. Bassianus, in the prime of youth, was the handsomest lad of his time. With physical beauty, bloom of youth, and splendor of attire combining to produce the same effect, the youth might well be compared to the handsome statues of Bacchus.

8 When Bassianus was performing his priestly duties, dancing about the altars in barbarian fashion to the music of flutes, pipes, and every kind of instrument, the natives and the soldiers watched him with more than ordinary curiosity, aware

9 that he belonged to the imperial family. His youthful beauty attracted the eyes of all. At that time a huge army was quartered at Emesa to guard Phoenicia. This army was later transferred from the city, as we shall relate in the pages to follow. The soldiers were therefore frequent visitors in the city and went to the temple on the pretext of worshiping the god; there they delighted in watching Bassianus. Some were deserters and compatriots of Maesa; while they stood admiring

10 the youth, Maesa, either inventing the story or telling the truth, informed them that Bassianus was really the son of Caracalla, although it might appear that he had another father. She claimed that when she was living in the palace with her sister, Caracalla slept with both of her daughters, who were young and beautiful. The men repeated her story to their fellow soldiers, and it soon became common knowl-

11 edge throughout the army. Maesa was rumored to be enormously wealthy, and it was reported that she would immediately give all her money to the soldiers if they restored the empire to her family. The soldiers agreed that if the family would come secretly to the camp at night, they would open the gates, receive the family inside, and proclaim Bassianus emperor and son of Caracalla. The old woman agreed to the plan, preferring to risk any danger rather than live

in obscurity and appear to have been discarded. And so she slipped unnoticed out of the city at night with her daughters and grandsons. Guided by soldiers who had deserted, they came to the wall of the camp and were warmly received inside. Immediately the entire army saluted Bassianus as "Son of Caracalla," and, wrapping him in a purple military cloak, held him inside the camp. Then, bringing in all the supplies from the villages and adjacent fields, together with the women and children, they prepared to endure a siege if it should prove necessary.

CHAPTER IV

THESE matters were reported to Macrinus while he was at Antioch, and the rumor quickly spread through the rest of the armies that the son of Caracalla had been found and that the sister of Julia was handing out money. Believing everything that was said and accepting it as true, the soldiers were deeply stirred. They were moved by hatred of Macrinus and pity for the memory of Caracalla; these considerations persuaded them to support a change of emperors. More than any other factor, however, the hope of money influenced their decision, and many soldiers voluntarily deserted to the new Caracalla. Contemptuously dismissing the affair as the efforts of children, and displaying his usual indolence, Macrinus remained at home, but he did send one of the praetorian prefects to Emesa with a contingent of troops which he considered large enough to crush the rebels with the greatest of ease. When Julianus (for this was the prefect's name) arrived and attacked the walls of the camp, the soldiers inside, mounting the towers and battlements, displayed Bassianus to the besieging army; cheering the son of Caracalla, they waved their full purses to induce the attackers to desert.

BOOK FIVE

4 Believing that Bassianus was the son of Caracalla and looked exactly like him (for this is what they wanted to see), the besieging soldiers cut off Julianus' head and sent it back to Macrinus; when the gates were opened, all of them were welcomed into the camp. The troops, thus augmented, were sufficient not only to withstand a siege but also to fight a pitched battle at close quarters. The number of those who deserted each day, though they came in small groups, continued to increase the size of the army in the camp.

5 When he learned of these developments, Macrinus assembled all the available troops and marched out to put under siege those who had deserted him for Elagabalus.[3] The soldiers of Elagabalus, however, did not wait for the attack. Finding his troops bold enough to march out confidently to engage
6 Macrinus in battle, the youth led them from the city. When the two armies met on the borders of Phoenicia and Syria, Elagabalus' soldiers fought with spirit, fearing that if they should lose, they would suffer for what they had done. The soldiers of Macrinus, on the other hand, were completely in-
7 different and deserted to Elagabalus. When Macrinus saw what was happening, he was afraid that, having lost all his troops, he would be captured and shamefully treated. While the battle was still raging, he stripped off his purple cloak and other imperial insignia and secretly left the field with a few centurions whom he believed to be especially loyal to him. To avoid recognition he shaved off his beard, donned
8 a traveling cloak, and kept his head covered. He traveled night and day and thus outdistanced the report of his disaster; the centurions drove the chariots at top speed, as if they had been sent by Macrinus, still emperor, on an urgent mission.

And so Macrinus fled from the battle. Both armies continued the fight; the bodyguards and spearbearers whom

---
[3] I have regularly substituted for "Antoninus" the more familiar "Elagabalus."

they call praetorians fought for Macrinus, these picked men making a courageous stand against the rest of the army; the remainder of the troops fought for Elagabalus. But when those who were fighting for Macrinus saw neither the emperor nor the imperial emblems for some time, they did not know whether he had been killed or had fled the battlefield, nor did they know what course they should follow under the circumstances. They had no desire to fight for a man who was absent, and were ashamed to surrender and, betrayed, become prisoners of war. Informed by deserters of Macrinus' flight, Elagabalus sent heralds to advise the praetorians that they were fighting vainly for a cowardly fugitive; he solemnly promised them security and amnesty, and offered them service as his bodyguard. Convinced, the praetorians switched their allegiance. Elagabalus then sent men in pursuit of Macrinus, who by that time had fled some distance. The fugitive was finally captured at Chalcedon in Bithynia, desperately ill and exhausted by his continuous flight. His pursuers found him hiding in the outskirts of the city and cut off his head. It is said that he was hurrying to Rome, putting his faith in the people's enthusiastic support; but when he attempted to cross over to Europe by the narrow Propontic Gulf and was already close to Byzantium, they say that the wind was against him and carried him back to Asia and his fate. So, by mischance, Macrinus failed to elude his pursuers and met an ignoble end a little later while striving to get to Rome, where he should have gone in the beginning. Thus he owed his downfall equally to bad judgment and bad luck.

Such was the fate of Macrinus; with him perished his son Diadumenianus, who was his Caesar.

CHAPTER V

NOW the entire army went over to Elagabalus, proclaiming him emperor, and the youth assumed control of the empire. After affairs in the East had been set in order for him by his grandmother and his advisers (for he was young in years, and lacking in education and administrative experience), he delayed his departure for only a short time, as Maesa was eager to return to her familiar imperial life at Rome. The senate and the Roman people were dismayed at the report of these developments, but submitted through necessity because the army had elected to follow this course. They attributed the affair to the indolence and weakness of Macrinus and said that he alone was responsible for what had happened.

Leaving Syria, Elagabalus proceeded to Nicomedia, where he was forced by the season of the year to spend the winter. Immediately he plunged into his mad activities, performing for his native god the fantastic rites in which he had been trained from childhood. He wore the richest clothing, draping himself in purple robes embroidered in gold; to his necklaces and bracelets he added a crown, a tiara glittering with gold and jewels. His dress showed the influence of the sacred robe of the Phoenicians and the luxurious garb of the Medes. He loathed Greek and Roman garments because they were made of wool, in his opinion an inferior material; only the Syrian cloth met with his approval. Accompanied by flutes and drums, he went about performing, as it appeared, orgiastic service to his god.

When she saw what Elagabalus was doing, Maesa was greatly disturbed and tried again and again to persuade the youth to wear Roman dress when he entered the city to visit the senate. She was afraid that his appearance, obviously foreign and wholly barbaric, would offend those who saw him; they were not used to such garb and considered his ornaments suitable only for women. But Elagabalus had nothing but contempt for the old woman's warnings, nor did anyone else succeed in convincing him. (He would listen only to those who were like him and flattered his faults.) Since, however, he wished the senate and the Roman people to grow accustomed to seeing him in this costume and wished to test their reaction to this exotic sight, before he returned to Rome he had a full-length portrait painted, showing him performing his priestly duties in public. His native god also appeared in the painting; the emperor was depicted sacrificing to him under favorable auspices. Elagabalus sent this picture to Rome to be hung in the center of the senate house, high above the statue of Victory before which each senator burns frankincense and pours a libation of wine upon entering the chamber. He directed all Roman officials who perform public sacrifices to call upon the new god Elagabalus before all the other gods whom they invoke in their rites. By the time the emperor came to Rome presenting the appearance described above, the Romans saw nothing unusual in it, for the painting had prepared them for what to expect. Elagabalus then made the distribution of money customary at the succession of an emperor and staged lavish and extravagant spectacles of every kind. He erected a huge and magnificent temple to his god and surrounded it with numerous altars. Coming forth early each morning, he sacrificed there hecatombs of bulls and a vast number of sheep. These he placed upon the altars and heaped up spices of every kind; he also set before the altars many jars of the oldest and finest wines, so that the streams of blood mingled with streams of wine. Elagabalus danced around the altars to music played on every kind of instrument; women from his own country accompanied him in these dances, carrying cymbals and drums as they

BOOK FIVE

circled the altars. The entire senate and all the knights stood watching, like spectators at the theater. The spices and entrails of the sacrificial animals were not carried by servants or men of low birth; rather, they were borne along in gold vessels held on high by the praetorian prefects and the most important magistrates, who wore long-sleeved robes with a broad purple stripe in the center, robes which hung to their feet in the Phoenician style. On their feet were the linen shoes customarily worn by the Eastern prophets. It was obvious that Elagabalus was paying the highest honor to those associated with him in the performance of the sacred rites.

CHAPTER VI

EVEN though the emperor seemed to be devoting all his attention to dancing and to his priestly duties, still he found time to execute many famous and wealthy men who were charged with ridiculing and censuring his way of life. He married one of the noblest of the Roman ladies and proclaimed her Augusta;[4] but he soon divorced her and, after depriving her of the imperial honors, ordered her to return to private life. So that he might seem to be doing something manly, he made love to one of the Vestal Virgins of Rome, priestesses who are bound by sacred vows to be chaste and remain virgin to the end of their lives; taking the maiden away from Vesta and the holy virgins' quarters, he made her his wife. He sent a letter to the senate asking to be forgiven his impious and adolescent transgression, telling them that he was afflicted with a masculine failing—an overwhelming passion for the maiden. He also informed them that the marriage of a priest and a priestess was both proper and sanctioned. But

---

[4] After the Flavian era this title was normally conferred upon the wife of the reigning emperor.

a short time later he divorced this girl and took yet a third wife, a girl who belonged to the family of Commodus.

Not content with making a mockery of human marriage, he even sought a wife for the god whose priest he was. He brought into his own bedroom the statue of Pallas which the Romans worship hidden and unseen. Even though this statue had not been moved from the time when it was first brought from Troy, except when the temple of Vesta was destroyed by fire, Elagabalus moved it now and brought it into the palace to be married to his god. But proclaiming that his god was not pleased by a goddess of war wearing full armor, he sent for the statue of Urania which the Carthaginians and Libyans especially venerate. This statue they say Dido the Phoenician set up at the time when she cut the hide into strips and founded the ancient city of Carthage. The Libyans call this goddess Urania, but the Phoenicians worship her as Astroarche, identifying her with the moon. Claiming that he was arranging a marriage of the sun and the moon, Elagabalus sent for the statue and all the gold in the temple and ordered the Carthaginians to provide, in addition, a huge sum of money for the goddess' dowry. When the statue arrived, he set it up with his god and ordered all men in Rome and throughout Italy to celebrate with lavish feasts and festivals, publicly and privately, in honor of the marriage of the deities.

In the suburbs of Rome the emperor built a very large and magnificent temple to which every year in midsummer he brought his god. He staged lavish shows and built race tracks and theaters, believing that chariot races, shows, and countless recitals would please the people, who held night-long feasts and celebrations. He placed the sun god in a chariot adorned with gold and jewels and brought him out from the city to the suburbs. A six-horse chariot bore the sun god, the

BOOK FIVE

horses huge and flawlessly white, with expensive gold fittings and rich ornaments. No one held the reins, and no one rode in the chariot; the vehicle was escorted as if the sun god himself were the charioteer. Elagabalus ran backward in front of the chariot, facing the god and holding the horses' reins. He made the whole journey in this reverse fashion, looking up into the face of his god. Since he was unable to see where he was going, his route was paved with gold dust to keep him from stumbling and falling, and bodyguards supported him on each side to protect him from injury. The people ran parallel to him, carrying torches and tossing wreaths and flowers. The statues of all the gods, the costly or sacred offerings in the temples, the imperial ornaments, and valuable heirlooms were carried by the cavalry and the entire Praetorian Guard in honor of the sun god. After thus bringing the god out and placing him in the temple, Elagabalus performed the rites and sacrifices described above; then, climbing to the huge, lofty towers which he had erected, he threw down, indiscriminately, cups of gold and silver, clothing, and cloth of every type to the mob below. He also distributed all kinds of tame animals except swine, which, in accordance with Phoenician custom, he shunned. Many lost their lives in the ensuing scramble, impaled on the soldiers' spears or trampled to death; thus the celebration of the emperor brought tragedy to a host of people. Elagabalus was often seen driving a chariot or dancing. He had no desire to sin in secret, but appeared in public with eyes painted and cheeks rouged; these cosmetics marred a face naturally handsome.

CHAPTER VII

OBSERVING his actions, Maesa suspected that the soldiers were outraged by his eccentricities. Fearing that if Elagabalus were killed, she would become a private citizen again, she tried to persuade the youth, who was in every respect an empty-headed young idiot, to adopt as his son and appoint as Caesar his first cousin and her grandson, the child of her other daughter, Mamaea. She told the emperor what it pleased him to hear, that it was clearly necessary for him to have time to attend to the worship and service of his god and to devote himself to the rites and revelries and divine functions, but that there should be another responsible for human affairs, to afford him leisure and freedom from the cares of empire. It was not necessary for him, she said, to look for a stranger or someone not a relative; he should entrust these duties to his own cousin. It was then that the name of Alexanius was changed to Alexander; the name of his grandfather became Alexander the Great, since the Macedonian was very famous and was held in high esteem by the alleged father of them both. Maesa's daughters, and the old woman too, boasted of their adultery with Caracalla, son of Severus, in order to increase the soldiers' love for the youths, who thus appeared to be Caracalla's sons.

Alexander was then appointed Caesar and served as consul with Elagabalus himself. Appearing before the senate, Elagabalus confirmed this appointment, and all the senators voted approval of the fantastic and ridiculous situation they were ordered to endorse—that the emperor, who was about sixteen, assume the role of father to Alexander, who was twelve. After adopting Alexander as Caesar, Elagabalus undertook to teach him his own practices; he instructed him in dancing and prancing, and, enrolling him in the priesthood, wanted the lad to imitate his appearance and actions. But his mother Mamaea kept Alexander from taking part in activities so disgraceful and unworthy of an emperor. Privately, she summoned teachers of every subject and had her son trained in the lessons of self-discipline; since he devoted himself to wrestling and to physical exercise as well, he was, by his mother's efforts, educated according to both the Greek and the Roman systems. Elagabalus, much annoyed at this, regretted his decision to make Alexander his son and partner in the empire. He therefore banished Alexander's teachers from the imperial palace; he put to death some of the most distinguished and sent others into exile. The emperor offered the most absurd excuses for doing this, claiming that these men, by teaching Alexander self-control, educating him in human affairs, and refusing to allow him to dance and take part in the frenzied orgies, would corrupt his adopted son. The madness of Elagabalus increased to such a degree that he appointed all the actors from the stage and the public theaters to the most important posts in the empire, selecting as his praetorian prefect a man who had from childhood danced publicly in the Roman theater. He elevated in similar fashion another young actor, putting him in charge of the education and conduct of the Roman youths and of the qualifications of those appointed to membership in the senatorial and Equestrian orders. To charioteers, comedians, and actors of mimes he entrusted the most important and responsible imperial posts. To slaves and freedmen, to men notorious for disgraceful acts, he assigned the proconsular provincial governorships.

CHAPTER VIII

WITH everything that formerly had been held sacred being done in a frenzy of arrogance and madness, all the Romans, especially the praetorians, were angered and disgusted. They were annoyed when they saw the emperor, his face painted more elaborately than that of any modest woman, dancing in luxurious robes and effeminately adorned with gold necklaces. As a result, they were more favorably disposed toward Alexander, for they expected great things of a lad so properly and modestly reared. They kept continual watch upon the youth when they saw that Elagabalus was plotting against him. His mother Mamaea did not allow her son to touch any food or drink sent by the emperor, nor did Alexander use the cupbearers or cooks employed in the palace or those who happened to be in their mutual service; only those chosen by his mother, those who seemed most trustworthy, were allowed to handle Alexander's food. Mamaea secretly distributed money to the praetorians to win their good will for her son; it was to gold that the praetorians were particularly devoted.

When he learned this, Elagabalus plotted against Alexander and his mother in every conceivable way, but Maesa, the grandmother of them both, foiled all his schemes; she was astute in every way and had spent much of her life in the imperial palace. As the sister of Severus' wife Julia, Maesa had always lived with the empress at the court. Therefore, none of Elagabalus' schemes escaped her attention, for the emperor was careless by nature, and his intrigues were always obvious. Since his plots failed, the emperor undertook to strip Alexander of the honor of Caesar, and the youth was no longer to be seen at public addresses or in public processions. But the soldiers called for Alexander and were angry because he had been removed from his imperial post. Elagabalus circulated a rumor that Alexander was dying, to see how the praetorians would react to the news. When they did not see the youth, the praetorians were deeply grieved and enraged by the report; they refused to send the regular contingent of guards to the emperor and remained in the camp, demanding to see Alexander in the temple there. Thoroughly frightened, Elagabalus placed Alexander in the imperial litter, which was richly decorated with gold and precious gems, and set out with him for the praetorian camp. The guards opened the gates and, receiving them inside, brought the two

BOOK FIVE

7 youths to the temple in the camp. They welcomed Alexander with enthusiastic cheers, but ignored the emperor. Fuming at this treatment, although he spent the night in the camp, Elagabalus unleashed the fury of his wrath against the praetorians. He ordered the arrest and punishment of the guards who had cheered Alexander openly and enthusiastically, pretending that these were responsible for the revolt and uproar.

8 The praetorians were enraged by this order; since they had other reasons, also, for hating Elagabalus, they wished now to rid themselves of so disgraceful an emperor, and believed, too, that they should rescue the praetorians under arrest. Considering the occasion ideal and the provocation just, they killed Elagabalus and his mother Soaemias (for she was in the camp as Augusta and as his mother), together with all his attendants who were seized in the camp and who

9 seemed to be his associates and companions in evil.[5] They gave the bodies of Elagabalus and Soaemias to those who wanted to drag them about and abuse them; when the bodies had been dragged throughout the city, the mutilated corpses were thrown into the public sewer which flows into the Tiber.

10 After having ruled the empire for more than five years, leading the kind of life described above, Elagabalus perished in this manner together with his mother. The praetorians then proclaimed Alexander emperor and conducted him into the palace while he was still a youth and still being given a thorough education by his mother and his grandmother.

---

[5] March 12, 222.

BOOK SIX

SEVERUS ALEXANDER

CHAPTER 1

THE fate which Elagabalus suffered I have described in the preceding pages. When Alexander received the empire, the appearance and the title of emperor were allowed him, but the management and control of imperial affairs were in the hands of his women, and they undertook a more moderate and more equitable administration. First, they chose from the senate, to be the emperor's advisory council, sixteen men who because of their age seemed most dignified and temperate in their conduct. Nothing was said or done unless these men had first considered the matter and given unanimous approval. The fact that the character of the imperial government was changed from an arrogant autocracy to a form of aristocracy pleased the people, the army, and especially the senators. To begin with, the statues of the gods which Elagabalus had moved or transferred were returned to their original positions in the ancient temples and shrines. The unqualified men whom Elagabalus had promoted to positions of trust or honor or who were notorious for their crimes were deprived of what they had received from the

BOOK SIX

emperor and were ordered by the councilors to return to their former occupations. In all government business and matters of state, the emperor's council entrusted political matters and public affairs to those who were competent lawyers and skillful orators, while they put in charge of military affairs experienced men who were skilled in the arts of war.

After the empire had been governed in this manner for some time, Maesa, then an old woman, died; receiving the imperial honors, she became, as the Romans believe, a deity. Now left alone with her son, Mamaea tried to govern and control him in the same fashion. Fearing that his vigorous young manhood might plunge him into the errors of adolescence because his power and position were assured, Mamaea kept the palace under close guard and allowed no one suspected of debauchery to approach the youth. She was afraid that his character would be corrupted if his flatterers aroused his growing appetites to disgraceful desires. She therefore induced him to serve as judge in the courts continually and for most of each day; occupied with important matters and the necessary business of the empire, he would have no opportunity to indulge in scandalous practices. Alexander's deportment was governed by a character naturally mild and civilized, and much inclined to benevolence, as was made clear when the youth grew older. At any rate, he entered the fourteenth year of his reign without bloodshed, and no one could say that the emperor had been responsible for anyone's murder. Even though men were convicted of serious crimes, he nevertheless granted them pardons to avoid putting them to death, and not readily did any emperor of our time, after the reign of Marcus, act in this way or display so much concern for human life. Indeed, over a period of many years, no one could recall that any man had been condemned to death by Alexander without a trial.

Alexander blamed his mother for her excessive love of

money and was annoyed by her relentless pursuit of gold. For a time she pretended to be gathering funds to enable Alexander to gratify the praetorians readily and generously, but in truth she was hoarding it for herself. And her miserliness in some measure reflected discredit upon his reign, even though he personally opposed it and was angry when she confiscated anyone's property and inheritance illegally.

Mamaea secured for Alexander a wife from the aristocracy. Although he loved the girl and lived with her, she was afterward banished from the palace by his mother, who, in her egotistic desire to be sole empress, envied the girl her title. So excessively arrogant did Mamaea become that the girl's father, though Alexander esteemed him highly, could no longer endure the woman's insolence toward him and his daughter; consequently, he took refuge in the praetorian camp, fully aware of the debt of gratitude he owed Alexander for the honors he had received from him, but complaining bitterly about Mamaea's insults. Enraged, Mamaea ordered him to be killed and at the same time drove the girl from the palace to exile in Libya. She did this against Alexander's wishes and in spite of his displeasure, but the emperor was dominated by his mother and obeyed her every command. One might bring this single charge against Alexander, that his excessive amiability and abnormal filial devotion led him to bow to his mother in matters he personally disapproved.

And so for thirteen years he ruled the empire in blameless fashion so far as he personally was concerned.

CHAPTER II

IN THE fourteenth year, however, unexpected dispatches from the governors of Syria and Mesopotamia revealed that Artaxerxes, the Persian king, had conquered the Parthi-

BOOK SIX

ans and seized their Eastern empire, killing Artabanus, who was formerly called the Great King and wore the double diadem. Artaxerxes then subdued all the barbarians on his borders and forced them to pay tribute. He did not remain quiet, however, nor stay on his side of the Tigris River, but, after scaling its banks and crossing the borders of the Roman empire, he overran Mesopotamia and threatened Syria. The entire continent opposite Europe, separated from it by

2 the Aegean Sea and the Propontic Gulf, and the region called Asia he wished to recover for the Persian empire. Believing these regions to be his by inheritance, he declared that all the countries in that area, including Ionia and Caria, had been ruled by Persian governors, beginning with Cyrus, who first made the Median empire Persian, and ending with Darius, the last of the Persian monarchs, whose kingdom was seized by Alexander the Great. He asserted that it was therefore proper for him to recover for the Persians the kingdom

3 which they had formerly possessed. When the Eastern governors revealed these developments in their dispatches, Alexander was greatly disturbed by these unanticipated tidings, particularly since, raised from childhood in an age of peace, he had spent his entire life in urban ease and comfort. Before doing anything else, he thought it best, after consulting his advisers, to send an embassy to the king and by his letters halt

4 the invasion and disappoint the barbarian's hopes. In these letters he told Artaxerxes that he must remain within his own borders and not initiate any action; let him not, deluded by vain hopes, stir up a great war, but rather let each of them be content with what was already his. Artaxerxes would find fighting against the Romans not the same thing as fighting with his barbarian kinsmen and neighbors. Alexander further reminded the Persian king of the victories won over them by Augustus, Trajan, Verus, and Severus. By writing letters of this kind, Alexander thought that he would

SEVERUS ALEXANDER

persuade the barbarian to remain quiet or frighten him to the same course. But Artaxerxes ignored Alexander's efforts; believing that the matter would be settled by arms, not by words, he took the field, pillaging and looting all the Roman provinces. He overran and plundered Mesopotamia, trampling it under the hoofs of his horses. He laid siege to the Roman garrison camps on the banks of the rivers, the camps which defended the empire. Rash by nature and elated by successes beyond his expectations, Artaxerxes was convinced that he could surmount every obstacle in his path. The considerations which led him to wish for an expanded empire were not small. He was the first Persian to dare to launch an attack on the Parthian empire and the first to succeed in winning back that empire for the Persians. Indeed, after Darius had been deprived of his kingdom by Alexander of Macedon, the Macedonians and Alexander's successors divided up the territory by countries and ruled the nations of the East and all Asia for many years. When these governors quarreled and the power of the Macedonians was weakened by continual wars, they say that Arsaces the Parthian was the first to persuade the barbarians in those regions to revolt from the Macedonians. Invested with the crown by the willing Parthians and the neighboring barbarians, Arsaces ruled as king. For a long time the empire remained in his own family, down to Artabanus in our time; then Artaxerxes killed Artabanus and took possession of his kingdom for the Persians. After easily subduing the neighboring barbarian nations, the king began to plot against the Roman empire.

CHAPTER III

WHEN the bold actions of this Eastern barbarian were disclosed to Alexander while he was passing the time in Rome, he found these affronts unendurable. Though the

BOOK SIX

undertaking distressed him and was contrary to his inclinations, since his governors there were calling for him, he made preparations for departure. He assembled for army service picked men from Italy and from all the Roman provinces, enrolling those whose age and physical condition qualified them for military service. The gathering of an army equal in size to the reported strength of the attacking barbarians caused the greatest upheaval throughout the Roman world. When these troops were gathered in Rome, Alexander ordered them to assemble on the usual plain. There he mounted a platform and addressed them as follows:

"I wished, fellow soldiers, to make the customary speech to you, the speech from which I, speaking to the popular taste, receive approval, and you, when you hear it, receive encouragement. Since you have now enjoyed many years of peace, you may be startled to hear something unusual or contrary to your anticipations. Brave and intelligent men should pray for things to turn out for the best, but they should also endure whatever befalls. It is true that the enjoyment of things done for pleasure brings gratification, but good repute results from the manliness involved in setting matters straight when necessity demands. To initiate unjust actions is not proof of good intentions, but it is a courageous deed to rid oneself of those who are troublesome if it is done with good conscience; one may expect good results if he has done nothing unjust but has avoided injustice. The Persian Artaxerxes has slain his master Artabanus, and the Parthian empire is now Persian. Despising our arms and contemptuous of the Roman reputation, Artaxerxes is attempting to overrun and destroy our imperial possessions. I first endeavored by letters and persuasion to check his mad greed and his lust for the property of others. But the king, with barbarian arrogance, is unwilling to remain within his own boundaries and challenges us to battle. Let us not hesitate to accept his

SEVERUS ALEXANDER

challenge. You veterans remind yourselves of the victories which you often won over the barbarians under the leadership of Severus and my father, Caracalla. You recruits, thirsting for glory and honor, make it clear that you know how to live at peace mildly and with propriety, but make it equally clear that you turn with courage to the tasks of war when necessity demands. The barbarian is bold against the hesitant and the cowardly, but he does not stand up in like fashion to those who fight back; it is not in close-quarter combat that they battle the enemy with hope of success. Rather, they believe that whatever success they win is the result of plundering after a feigned retreat and flight. Discipline and organized battle tactics favor us, together with the fact that we have always been taught to conquer the barbarian."

CHAPTER IV

WHEN Alexander finished speaking, the cheering army promised its wholehearted support for the war. After a lavish distribution of money to the soldiers, the emperor ordered preparations for his departure from the city. He then went before the senate and made a speech similar to the one recorded above; following this, he publicly announced his plans to march out. On the appointed day, after he had performed the sacrifices prescribed for departures, Alexander left Rome, weeping and repeatedly looking back at the city. The senate and all the people escorted him, and everyone wept, for he was held in great affection by the people of Rome, among whom he had been reared and whom he had ruled with moderation for many years. Traveling rapidly, he came to Antioch, after visiting the provinces and the garrison camps in Illyricum; from that region he collected a huge force of troops. While in Antioch he continued

BOOK SIX

his preparations for the war, giving the soldiers military training under field conditions.

4 He thought it best to send another embassy to the Persian king to discuss the possibility of peace and friendship, hoping to persuade him or to intimidate him by his presence. The barbarian, however, sent the envoys back to the emperor unsuccessful. Then Artaxerxes chose four hundred very tall Persians, outfitted them with fine clothes and gold ornaments, and equipped them with horses and bows; he sent these men to Alexander as envoys, thinking that their ap-
5 pearance would dazzle the Romans. The envoys said that the great king Artaxerxes ordered the Romans and their emperor to withdraw from all Syria and from that part of Asia opposite Europe; they were to permit the Persians to rule as far as Ionia and Caria and to govern all the nations separated by the Aegean Sea and the Propontic Gulf, inasmuch as
6 these were the Persians' by right of inheritance. When the Persian envoys delivered these demands, Alexander ordered the entire four hundred to be arrested; stripping off their finery, he sent the group to Phrygia, where villages and farm land were assigned to them, but he gave orders that they were not to be allowed to return to their native country. He treated them in this fashion because he thought it dishonorable and cowardly to put them to death, since they were not fighting but simply carrying out their master's orders.
7 This is the way the affair turned out. While Alexander was preparing to cross the Tigris and Euphrates rivers and lead his army into barbarian territory, several mutinies broke out among his troops, especially among the soldiers from Egypt; but revolts occurred also in Syria, where the soldiers attempted to proclaim a new emperor. These defections were quickly discovered and suppressed. At this time Alexander transferred to other stations those field armies which seemed better able to check the barbarian invasions.

CHAPTER V

AFTER thus setting matters in order, Alexander, considering that the huge army he had assembled was now nearly equal in power and numbers to the barbarians, consulted his advisers and then divided his force into three separate armies. One army he ordered to overrun the land of the Medes after marching north and passing through Armenia, which seemed to favor the Roman cause. He sent the second army to the eastern sector of the barbarian territory, where, it is said, the Tigris and Euphrates rivers at their confluence empty into very dense marshes; these are the only rivers whose mouths cannot be clearly determined. The third and most powerful army he kept himself, promising to lead it against the barbarians in the central sector. He thought that in this way he would attack them from different directions when they were unprepared and not anticipating such strategy, and he believed that the Persian horde, constantly split up to face their attackers on several fronts, would be weaker and less unified for battle. The barbarians, it may be noted, do not hire mercenary soldiers as the Romans do, nor do they maintain trained standing armies. Rather, all the available men, and sometimes the women too, mobilize at the king's order. At the end of the war each man returns to his regular occupation, taking as his pay whatever falls to his lot from the general booty. They use the bow and the horse in war, as the Romans do, but the barbarians are reared with these from childhood, and live by hunting; they never lay aside their quivers or dismount from their horses, but employ them constantly for war and the chase.

Alexander therefore devised what he believed to be the best possible plan of action, only to have Fortune defeat his design. The army sent through Armenia had an agonizing

BOOK SIX

passage over the high, steep mountains of that country. (As it was still summer, however, they were able to complete the crossing.) Then, plunging down into the land of the Medes, the Roman soldiers devastated the countryside, burning many villages and carrying off much loot. Informed of this, the Persian king led his army to the aid of the Medes, but met with little success in his efforts to halt the Roman
6 advance. This is rough country; while it provided firm footing and easy passage for the infantry, the rugged mountain terrain hampered the movements of the barbarian cavalry and prevented their riding down the Romans or even making contact with them. Then men came and reported to the Persian king that another Roman army had appeared in
7 eastern Parthia and was overrunning the plains there. Fearing that the Romans, after ravaging Parthia unopposed, might advance into Persia, Artaxerxes left behind a force which he thought strong enough to defend Media, and hurried with his entire army into the eastern sector. The Romans were advancing much too carelessly because they had met no opposition and, in addition, they believed that Alexander and his army, the largest and most formidable of the three, had already attacked the barbarians in the central sector. They thought, too, that their own advance would be easier and less hazardous when the barbarians were constantly being drawn off elsewhere to meet the threat of the emperor's
8 army. All three Roman armies had been ordered to invade the enemy's territory, and a final rendezvous had been selected to which they were to bring their booty and prisoners. But Alexander failed them: he did not bring his army or come himself into barbarian territory, either because he was afraid to risk his life for the Roman empire or because his mother's feminine fears or excessive mother love restrained
9 him. She blocked his efforts at courage by persuading him that he should let others risk their lives for him, but that

SEVERUS ALEXANDER

he should not personally fight in battle. It was this reluctance of his which led to the destruction of the advancing Roman army. The king attacked it unexpectedly with his entire force and trapped the Romans like fish in a net; firing their arrows from all sides at the encircled soldiers, the Persians massacred the whole army. The outnumbered Romans were unable to stem the attack of the Persian horde; they used their shields to protect those parts of their bodies exposed to the Persian arrows. Content merely to protect themselves, they offered no resistance. As a result, all the Romans were driven into one spot, where they made a wall of their shields and fought like an army under siege. Hit and wounded from every side, they held out bravely as long as they could, but in the end all were killed. The Romans suffered a staggering disaster; it is not easy to recall another like it, one in which a great army was destroyed, an army inferior in strength and determination to none of the armies of old. The successful outcome of these important events encouraged the Persian king to anticipate better things in the future.

CHAPTER VI

WHEN the disaster was reported to Alexander, who was seriously ill either from despondency or the unfamiliar air, he fell into despair. The rest of the army angrily denounced the emperor because the invading army had been destroyed as a result of his failure to carry out the plans faithfully agreed upon. And now Alexander refused to endure his indisposition and the stifling air any longer. The entire army was sick and the troops from Illyricum especially were seriously ill and dying, being accustomed to moist, cool air and to more food than they were being issued. Eager to set out for Antioch, Alexander ordered the army in Media to proceed to that city. This army, in its advance, was almost

BOOK SIX

totally destroyed in the mountains; a great many soldiers suffered mutilation in the frigid country, and only a handful of the large number of troops who started the march managed to reach Antioch. The emperor led his own large force to that city, and many of them perished too; so the affair brought the greatest discontent to the army and the greatest dishonor to Alexander, who was betrayed by bad luck and bad judgment. Of the three armies into which he had divided his total force, the greater part was lost by various misfortunes—disease, war, and cold.

4 In Antioch, Alexander was quickly revived by the cool air and good water of that city after the acrid drought in Mesopotamia, and the soldiers too recovered there. The emperor tried to console them for their sufferings by a lavish distribution of money, in the belief that this was the only way he could regain their good will. He assembled an army and prepared to march against the Persians again if they should 5 give trouble and not remain quiet. But it was reported that Artaxerxes had disbanded his army and sent each soldier back to his own country. Though the barbarians seemed to have conquered because of their superior strength, they were exhausted by the numerous skirmishes in Media and by the battle in Parthia, where they lost many killed and many wounded. The Romans were not defeated because they were cowards; indeed, they did the enemy much damage and 6 lost only because they were outnumbered. Since the total number of troops which fell on both sides was virtually identical, the surviving barbarians appeared to have won, but by superior numbers, not by superior power. It is no little proof of how much the barbarians suffered that for three or four years after this they remained quiet and did not take up arms. All this the emperor learned while he was at Antioch. Relieved of anxiety about the war, he grew more

SEVERUS ALEXANDER

cheerful and less apprehensive and devoted himself to enjoying the pleasures which the city offered.

CHAPTER VII

ALEXANDER did not believe that Persian affairs would remain permanently quiet and peaceful, but he did think that the barbarian had provided him with a temporary respite from campaigning. The barbarian army, once disbanded, was not easily remustered, as it was not organized on a permanent basis. More a mob than a regular army, the soldiers had only those supplies which each man brought for himself when he reported for duty. Moreover, the Persians are reluctant to leave their wives, children, and homeland. Now unexpected messages and dispatches upset Alexander and caused him even greater anxiety: the governors in Illyria reported that the Germans had crossed the Rhine and the Danube rivers, were plundering the Roman empire, and with a huge force were overrunning the garrison camps on the banks of these rivers, as well as the cities and villages there. They reported also that the provinces of Illyricum bordering on and close to Italy were in danger. The governors informed the emperor that it was absolutely necessary that he and his entire army come to them. The revelation of these developments terrified Alexander and aroused great concern among the soldiers from Illyricum, who seemed to have suffered a double disaster; the men who had undergone many hardships in the Persian expedition now learned that their families had been slaughtered by the Germans. They were naturally enraged at this, and blamed Alexander for their misfortunes because he had betrayed affairs in the East by his cowardice and carelessness and was hesitant and dilatory about the situation in the North. Alexander and his ad-

BOOK SIX

visers, too, feared for the safety of Italy itself. They did not consider the Persian threat at all similar to the German. The fact is that those who live in the East, separated from the West by a great continent and a broad sea, scarcely ever hear of Italy, whereas the provinces of Illyricum, since they are narrow and very little of their territory is under Roman control, make the Germans actually neighbors of the Italians;
5 the two peoples thus share common borders. Although he loathed the idea, Alexander glumly announced his departure for Illyria. Necessity compelled him to go, however; and so, leaving behind a force which he considered strong enough to defend the Roman frontiers, after he had seen to the forts and the walls of the camps with greater care and had assigned to each fort its normal complement of troops, the emperor marched out against the Germans with the rest of his army.
6 Completing the journey quickly, he encamped on the banks of the Rhine and made preparations for the German campaign. Alexander spanned the river with boats lashed together to form a bridge, thinking that this would provide an easy means of crossing for his soldiers. The Rhine in Germany and the Danube in Pannonia are the largest of the northern rivers. In summer their depth and width make them easily navigable, but in the cold winters they freeze over and appear like a level plain which can be crossed on horse-
7 back. The river becomes so firm and solid in that season that it supports horses and men. Then those who want drinking water do not come to the river with pitchers and bowls; they bring axes and mattocks and, when they have finished chopping, take up water without using bowls and carry it in chunks as hard as rock.
8   Such is the nature of these rivers. Alexander had brought with him many Moroccan javelin men and a huge force of archers from the East and from the Osroenian country, together with Parthian deserters and mercenaries who had

SEVERUS ALEXANDER

offered their help; with these he prepared to battle the Germans. The missile men were especially troublesome to the Germans: the Moroccans hurl their javelins from a distance and attack and retreat nimbly, while the archers, far removed from their targets, easily fire their arrows into the bare heads and huge bodies of the Germans; but when the Germans attacked at full speed and fought hand to hand, they were often the equal of the Romans.

Alexander was thus occupied with these matters. He thought it wise, however, to send an embassy to the Germans to discuss the possibilities of a peaceful settlement. He promised to give them everything they asked and to hand over a large amount of money. The avaricious Germans are susceptible to bribes and are always ready to sell peace to the Romans for gold. Consequently, Alexander undertook to buy a truce rather than risk the hazards of war. The soldiers, however, were not pleased by his action, for the time was passing without profit to them, and Alexander was doing nothing courageous or energetic about the war; on the contrary, when it was essential that he march out and punish the Germans for their insults, he spent the time in chariot racing and luxurious living.

CHAPTER VIII

THERE was in the Roman army a man named Maximinus whose half-barbarian family lived in a village in the most remote section of Thrace. They say that as a boy he was a shepherd, but that in his youthful prime he was drafted into the cavalry because of his size and strength. After a short time, favored by Fortune, he advanced through all the military ranks, rising eventually to the command of armies and the governing of provinces. Because of his military experience, which I have noted above, Alexander put

BOOK SIX

Maximinus in charge of training recruits for the entire army; his task was to instruct them in military duties and prepare them for service in war. By carrying out his assignments thoroughly and diligently, Maximinus won the affection of the soldiers. He not only taught them their duties; he also demonstrated personally to each man what he was to do. As a result, the recruits imitated his manliness and were both his pupils and his admirers. He won their devotion by giving them all kinds of gifts and rewards. Consequently, the recruits, who included an especially large number of Pannonians, praised the masculinity of Maximinus and despised Alexander as a mother's boy. Their contempt for the emperor was increased by the fact that the empire was being managed by a woman's authority and a woman's judgment, and by the fact that Alexander had directed the campaigns carelessly and timidly. They reminded each other of the defeats in the East which had resulted from the emperor's negligence and of his failure to do anything courageous or vigorous when he faced the Germans. The soldiers were therefore ready for a change of emperors. They had additional reasons for discontent: they considered the current reign burdensome because of its long duration; they thought it profitless for them now that all rivalry had been eliminated; and they hoped that the reign which they intended to institute would be advantageous to them and that the empire would be much coveted and highly valued by a man who received it unexpectedly. They plotted now to kill Alexander and proclaim Maximinus emperor and Augustus, since he was their fellow soldier and messmate and seemed, because of his experience and courage, to be the right man to take charge of the present war. They therefore assembled on the drill field for their regular training; when Maximinus took his position before them, either unaware of what was happening or having secretly made prior preparations for the event, the

soldiers robed him in the imperial purple and proclaimed
him emperor. At first he refused the honor and threw off the
purple, but when they pressed him and, waving their swords,
threatened to kill him, he preferred the future risk to the
present danger and accepted the empire; often before, he
said, dreams and prophecies had predicted this good fortune.
He told the soldiers, however, that he accepted the honor
unwillingly; he did not really want it and was simply obeying their wish in the matter. He then directed the soldiers
to put their thoughts into action, to take up arms and hurry
off to attack Alexander while he was still unaware of what
had happened. By reaching the emperor before the news of
their approach came, they would surprise his soldiers and his
bodyguards too. They would either persuade Alexander's
forces to join them, or would overcome them with no difficulty, since the imperial forces would be unprepared and
anticipating nothing of this nature. After arousing great
enthusiasm and good will among the troops, Maximinus
doubled their rations, promised them lavish gifts, and re-
voked all sentences and punishments. He then marched out,
for his camp was not far from the headquarters of Alexander
and his companions.

CHAPTER IX

WHEN these developments were reported, Alexander, panic-stricken by the incredible nature of the
message, was in complete confusion. Bursting from the imperial headquarters as if possessed, weeping and trembling, he
denounced Maximinus for his disloyalty and ingratitude, and
listed all the favors he had done the man. He castigated the
recruits for their recklessness and promised to give them
everything they asked and to set straight anything that dis-
pleased them. The soldiers guarding the emperor on that

BOOK SIX

day cheered his words; forming an escort, they promised
3 to defend him to the death. When the night had passed, men
came at dawn to report that Maximinus was approaching;
they said that a cloud of dust could be seen in the distance,
and the shouting of a huge throng was audible. Then Alexander came again to the drill field, summoned his troops, and
begged them to fight to preserve the life of a man whom
they had reared and under whose rule they had lived well
content for fourteen years. After this effort to move the soldiers to compassion, Alexander ordered them to take up arms
4 and go forth to battle. At first the soldiers obeyed him, but
they soon left the field and refused to fight. Some demanded
for execution the commanding general of the army and Alexander's associates, pretending that they were responsible for
the revolt. Others condemned the emperor's greedy mother
for cutting off their money, and despised Alexander for his
5 pettiness and stinginess in the matter of gifts. For a time
they did nothing but shout this barrage of charges. When the
army of Maximinus came into view, the clamoring recruits
called upon Alexander's soldiers to desert the miserly woman
and the timid, mother-dominated youth; at the same time
they urged his soldiers to join them in supporting a brave
and intelligent man, a fellow soldier who was always under
arms and busy with military matters. Convinced, Alexander's troops deserted him for Maximinus, who was then
6 proclaimed emperor by all. Trembling with fear, Alexander
was scarcely able to retire to his quarters. Clinging to his
mother and, as they say, complaining and lamenting that
she was to blame for his death, he awaited his executioner.
After being saluted as emperor by the entire army, Maximinus sent a tribune and several centurions to kill Alexander and his mother, together with any of his followers who
7 opposed them. When these men came to the emperor's quarters, they rushed in and killed him with his mother; they

SEVERUS ALEXANDER

also cut down those whom he had honored or who appeared to be his friends. Some, however, managed to flee or to hide for the moment, but Maximinus soon rounded up these fugitives and put them to death.

Such was the fate suffered by Alexander and his mother [A.D. 235] after he had ruled fourteen years without blame or bloodshed so far as it affected his subjects. A stranger to savagery, murder, and illegality, he was noted for his benevolence and good deeds. It is therefore entirely possible that the reign of Alexander might have won renown for its perfection had not his mother's petty avarice brought disgrace upon him.

BOOK SEVEN

MAXIMINUS AND THE GORDIANS

CHAPTER I

THE kind of life which Alexander led and the fate which overtook him after fourteen years as emperor we have described in the preceding book. When he assumed control of the empire, Maximinus reversed the situation, using his power savagely to inspire great fear. He undertook to substitute for a mild and moderate rule an autocracy in every way barbarous, well aware of the hostility directed toward him because he was the first man to rise from a lowly station to the post of highest honor. His character was naturally barbaric, as his race was barbarian. He had inherited the brutal disposition of his countrymen, and he intended to make his imperial position secure by acts of cruelty, fearing that he would become an object of contempt to the senate and the people, who might be more conscious of his lowly origin than impressed by the honor he had won. Everyone knew and spread the story that when he was a shepherd in the mountains of Thrace, he enlisted in a local auxiliary cohort be-

MAXIMINUS AND THE GORDIANS

cause of his huge size and great strength, and by luck became the emperor of the Romans. He therefore immediately disposed of Alexander's friends and associates, together with his senatorial advisers. Some he returned to Rome; others he dismissed for administrative reasons, in order to gain sole command of the army. He wanted no one around him who was superior to him in birth, desiring to act the tyrant as if from a lofty height, with no one near to whom he must defer. He banished from the imperial palace the entire band of attendants who had served Alexander for many years; he put most of them to death, suspecting that they were plotting against him, for he knew that they were still grieving over Alexander's assassination.

Maximinus was aroused to even greater fury by a plot allegedly formed by many centurions and all the senators. A man of the nobility and consular rank named Magnus was accused of organizing a conspiracy against the emperor and persuading some of the soldiers to transfer the empire to his charge. The plot was said to be something like this. Maximinus had bridged the Rhine River and was about to cross over and attack the Germans; for, as soon as he got control of the empire, he immediately began military operations. Since it appeared that he had been chosen emperor because of his great size, military prowess, and experience in war, he undertook to confirm by action the good reputation and high esteem he enjoyed among the soldiers. In this way, too, he tried to demonstrate that the charges of vacillation and timidity in military matters they brought against Alexander were well founded. Therefore he did not halt the soldiers' training and exercises, and remained under arms himself, spurring the army to action. Now, with the bridge completed, he was about to cross over to attack the Germans. Magnus, however, was said to have persuaded a few prominent soldiers, particularly those assigned to guard and main-

BOOK SEVEN

tain the bridge, to destroy the structure after Maximinus had crossed, and to betray the emperor to the barbarians by cutting off his only return route. After the bridge had been destroyed, the great river, very wide and deep, would be impassable, as no boats were available on the enemy's side. Such was the report of the plot, but whether it was actually true or whether it was fabricated by Maximinus it is not easy to say, because the matter was not investigated. Maximinus did not bring the conspirators to trial or allow them an opportunity to defend themselves; he arrested without warning all who were suspected and executed them without mercy.

There was now unrest among the Osroenian archers. These troops were much grieved by Alexander's death, and when they chanced to discover one of the emperor's friends, a former consul (a man named Quartinus, whom Maximinus had dismissed from the army), they seized him unexpectedly and made him their unwilling general; then, conferring upon him the purple and the processional fire, fatal honors, they brought to the imperial throne a most reluctant occupant. While Quartinus was asleep in his tent, a plot was formed against him, and he was assassinated during the night by a companion and presumed friend, a former commander of the Osroenians (his name was Macedon); yet this same Macedon had been a ringleader in the elevation of Quartinus to the throne and in the revolt against Maximinus; in both actions he had the full support of the Osroenians. Although he had no reason for enmity or hatred, Macedon killed the man whom he himself had chosen and persuaded to accept the empire. Thinking that this act would win him great favor with Maximinus, Macedon cut off Quartinus' head and brought it to the emperor. When he learned of the deed, Maximinus, though he believed that he had been freed from a dangerous enemy, nevertheless had Macedon killed, when the man had every reason to hope and believe that he would receive a generous reward. Macedon was not only the instigator of the revolt and the assassin of the man whom he had persuaded to accept the throne against his better judgment, but he was also a traitor to his friend.

For these reasons Maximinus was aroused to greater cruelty and more savage acts, and he was by nature inclined to such behavior. The emperor's appearance was frightening and his body was huge; not easily would any of the skilled Greek athletes or the best-trained warriors among the barbarians prove his equal.

CHAPTER II

HAVING settled affairs in the manner described above, Maximinus led out his entire army and crossed the bridge fearlessly, eager to do battle with the Germans. Under his command was a vast number of men, virtually the entire Roman military force, together with many Moroccan javelin men and Osroenian and Armenian archers; some were subject peoples, others friends and allies, and included, too, were a number of Parthian mercenaries and slaves captured by the Romans. This enormous force was originally assembled by Alexander, but it was increased in size and trained for service by Maximinus. The javelin men and archers seemed to be especially effective against the Germans, taking them by surprise, attacking with agility and then retreating without difficulty. Though he was in enemy territory, Maximinus advanced for a considerable distance because all the barbarians had fled and he met no opposition. He therefore laid waste the whole country, taking particular care to destroy the ripening grain, and burned the villages after allowing the army to plunder them. Fire destroys the German towns and houses very quickly. Although there is a scarcity of stone and fired brick in Germany, the forests are

BOOK SEVEN

dense, and timber is so abundant that they build their houses of wood, fitting and joining the squared beams. Maximinus advanced deep into German territory, carrying off booty and turning over to the army all the herds they encountered. The Germans had left the plains and treeless areas and were hiding in the forests; they remained in the woods and marshes so that the battle would have to take place where the thick screen of trees made the missiles and javelins of their enemies ineffectual and where the depths of the marshes were dangerous to the Romans because of their unfamiliarity with the region. The Germans, on the contrary, were well acquainted with the terrain and knew which places provided firm footing and which were impassable. They moved rapidly and easily through the marshes, in water only knee-deep. The Germans, who do all their bathing in the rivers, are expert swimmers.

As a result, most of the skirmishing occurred in those regions, and it was there that the emperor personally and very boldly joined battle. When the Germans rushed into a vast swamp in an effort to escape and the Romans hesitated to leap in after them in pursuit, Maximinus plunged into the marsh, though the water was deeper than his horse's belly; there he cut down the barbarians who opposed him. Then the rest of the army, ashamed to betray their emperor who was doing their fighting for them, took courage and leaped into the marsh behind him. A large number of men fell on both sides, but, while many Romans were killed, virtually the entire barbarian force was annihilated, and the emperor was the foremost man on the field. The swamp pool was choked with bodies, and the marsh ran red with blood; this land battle had all the appearance of a naval encounter. This engagement and his own bravery Maximinus reported in dispatches to the senate and Roman people; moreover, he ordered the scene to be painted on huge canvases to be set up in front of the senate house, so that the Romans might not only hear about the battle but also be able to see what happened there. Later the senate removed this picture together with the rest of his emblems of honor. Other battles took place in which Maximinus won praise for his personal participation, for fighting with his own hands, and for being in every conflict the best man on the field. After taking many German prisoners and seizing much booty, the emperor, since winter had already begun, went to Pannonia and spent his time at Sirmium, the largest city in that country; there he made preparations for his spring offensive. He threatened (and was determined) to defeat and subjugate the German nations as far as the ocean.

CHAPTER III

THIS is the kind of military man the emperor was, and his actions would have added to his reputation if he had not been much too ruthless and severe toward his associates and subjects. What profit was there in killing barbarians when greater slaughter occurred in Rome and the provinces? Or in carrying off booty captured from the enemy when he robbed his fellow countrymen of all their property? Complete indulgence—encouragement, I should say—was granted to informers to threaten and insult, and to reopen any known crimes committed by a man's ancestors which were hitherto unexposed and undetected. Anyone who was merely summoned into court by an informer was immediately judged guilty, and left with all his property confiscated. It was thus possible every day to see men who yesterday had been rich, today reduced to paupers, so great was the avarice of the tyrant, who pretended to be insuring a continuous supply of money for the soldiers. The emperor's ears were always open to slanderous charges, and he spared neither age nor position.

BOOK SEVEN

He arrested on slight and trivial charges many men who had governed provinces and commanded armies, who had won the honor of a consulship, or had gained fame by military
4 victories. He ordered these men to be brought in chariots to Pannonia, where he was then passing the time; they were to travel day and night, without an escort, from the east, the west, and the south, wherever they happened to be. After insulting and torturing these prisoners, he condemned them to exile or death.

As long as his actions affected only individuals and the calamities suffered were wholly private, the people of the cities and provinces were not particularly concerned with
5 what the emperor was doing. Unpleasant things which happen to those who seem to be fortunate or wealthy are not only a matter of indifference to the mob, but they often bring pleasure to mean and malicious men, who envy the powerful and the prosperous. After Maximinus had impoverished most of the distinguished men and confiscated their estates, which he considered small and insignificant and not sufficient for his purposes, he turned to the public treasuries; all the funds which had been collected for the citizens' welfare or for gifts, all the funds being held in reserve for shows or festivals, he transferred to his own personal fortune. The offerings which belonged to the temples, the statues of the gods, the tokens of honor of the heroes, the decorations on public buildings, the adornments of the city, in short, any material suitable for making coins, he handed over to the
6 mints. But what especially irked the people and aroused public indignation was the fact that, although no fighting was going on and no enemy was under arms anywhere, Rome appeared to be a city under siege. Some citizens, with angry shaking of fists, set guards around the temples, preferring to die before the altars than to stand by and see their country ravaged. From that time on, particularly in the cities

MAXIMINUS AND THE GORDIANS

and the provinces, the hearts of the people were filled with rage. The soldiers too were disgusted with his activities, for their relatives and fellow citizens complained that Maximinus was acting solely for the benefit of the military.

CHAPTER IV

FOR these reasons, and justifiably, the people were aroused to hatred and thoughts of revolt. Prayers were offered by all, and the outraged gods were invoked, but no one dared to start anything until, after Maximinus had completed three years as emperor, the people of Africa first took up arms and touched off a serious revolt for one of those trivial reasons which often prove fatal to a tyrant. The uprising occurred in this manner. The procurator of Africa was a man who performed his duties with excessive severity; he handed down extremely harsh decisions and extorted money to win the emperor's favor. Maximinus always appointed men who subscribed to his way of thinking. The treasury officials at that time, even if they happened to be honest, which was rarely the case, since they foresaw their own risks and knew the emperor's avarice, acted as dishonestly as the rest, even if they did so against their will. Then the procurator of Africa, who acted the tyrant with everyone, involved in lawsuits some young men of the wealthiest and most aristocratic local families and undertook to extort money from them and rob them of their inheritances. Angered by this, the youths promised to pay him the money, but requested a delay of a few days. Calling a meeting, they won the support of all who were known to have suffered an injury or feared that they might suffer one. They ordered the field laborers to come into the city at night armed with clubs and axes. Obeying their masters' orders, the workmen entered the city in a body before daybreak, carrying arms for

BOOK SEVEN

hand-to-hand fighting hidden under their clothes. A large number assembled; for Africa, which is a heavily populated province, has many farmers. When dawn was approaching, the youths appeared and ordered the mob of workmen to follow them as if they were simply part of the crowd; they directed the workmen to take their assigned positions and, keeping their weapons hidden, to resist bravely if any of the soldiers or the people should attack them to avenge the deed they were plotting. Carrying daggers under their robes, the youths approached the procurator as if to discuss the payment of the money; then, attacking him suddenly, they stabbed and killed him. When his bodyguards drew their swords in retaliation, the workmen from the fields pulled out their clubs and axes and, fighting for their masters, easily routed their opponents.

CHAPTER V

THE success of their plan immediately put the youths in a desperate situation; they realized that a single avenue of safety lay open to them: to add to their bold act deeds even bolder and, enlisting the governor of the province as a partner in their peril, to rouse the whole province to revolt. They knew that the governor, who hated Maximinus, had long prayed for this, but was afraid to act. As it was now noon, the entire group went to the house of the proconsul. The governor, whose name was Gordian, had received the African post by lot when he was about eighty years old, after he had previously governed many provinces and served in the highest public offices. For this reason the youths believed that he would accept with pleasure the office of emperor as the crowning achievement in his career in public office; they thought that the senate and the Roman people would be glad to accept as emperor a man from the aristoc-

MAXIMINUS AND THE GORDIANS

racy who had risen to the high office after many governorships as if in a regular *cursus*. It happened that on the day these events occurred Gordian was at home resting, enjoying a brief respite from his labors and duties. Accompanied by the entire band with drawn swords, the youths overpowered the guards on duty at the gates and burst into the house, where they found Gordian resting on a couch. Standing around him, they draped him in a purple cloak and greeted him with the imperial honors. Astounded by this unexpected turn of events, and thinking it was an act of treachery or part of a plot against him, Gordian threw himself to the floor, begging them to spare the life of an old man who had never harmed them and to continue to display their loyalty and good will toward the emperor. But the youths were insistent and drew their swords. Gordian, alarmed and unaware of what had occurred, did not understand the situation. One of the youths, a talented speaker of distinguished family, asked for quiet and ordered the rest to remain silent. Then, sword in hand, he addressed Gordian as follows: "With two dangers threatening you, the one present, the other future, the one already obvious, the other a remote possibility, you must make your choice whether to enjoy safety with us and have faith in greater things to come, in which indeed we have all placed our trust, or to die at our hands this very moment. If you elect to accept the present situation, there are many factors which augur well for the future: Maximinus' hatred of everyone; the people's longing for deliverance from a cruel tyrant; their approval of your conduct in your former offices; and the fact that among the senate and the Roman people you enjoy a distinguished reputation and are held in high esteem. But death awaits you this very day if you decide against us and refuse to join us, and we shall die ourselves, if need be, after we have killed you. We have done a deed which calls for even more desperate measures.

BOOK SEVEN

The tyrant's procurator is dead, having paid the penalty for his savagery—death at our hands. If you join us and share our peril you will enjoy the honor of being emperor, and the deed which we have done will be praised, not punished."

7 After the young man had finished speaking, the rest of the band cast aside all restraint. The entire populace of the city quickly assembled when the news was known, and the youths proclaimed Gordian Augustus. He begged to be excused, protesting that he was too old. But otherwise he was eager for fame, and did not enter into the office without some personal satisfaction, choosing to risk the future rather than the present danger, and thinking that it was not so terrible a thing to die, if need be, amidst the imperial honors.

8 Immediately the whole province of Africa was aroused; the people there pulled down Maximinus' emblems of honor and decorated their cities with paintings and statues of Gordian; they added "Africanus" to his imperial titles, giving him their own name, for the Libyans are called Africans in Latin.

CHAPTER VI

THESE events occurred at Thystrum, where Gordian was staying at the time. After a few days, however, he left that city, having assumed the title and appearance of emperor, and proceeded to Carthage, which he knew to be a large and heavily populated city where he might do everything just as if he were in Rome. The city of Carthage, in size, wealth, and population, is surpassed only by Rome and contends with Alexandria in Egypt for second place in the

2 empire. Gordian was accompanied by the entire imperial escort, the soldiers on duty there, and the tallest of the city's youths, who preceded him in the manner of the praetorians at Rome. The fasces were wreathed with laurel; it is the laurel which distinguishes the fasces of the emperor from

those of other officials. The sacred fire was carried before him, and for a brief period Carthage was Rome in appearance and prosperity.

Gordian wrote letters to all the prominent men in Rome, including the leading senators, most of whom were his friends and relatives. He sent open letters to the senate and the Roman people in which he revealed his union with the Africans and attacked the savagery of Maximinus, knowing that this trait of the emperor's character was most violently hated. He promised the Romans moderation in all things: he would banish informers, provide new trials for the unjustly condemned, and return exiles to their own lands. To the praetorians he promised more money than anyone had given them before, and he announced gifts for the people. Arrangements were made for the early execution of the commandant of the Praetorian Guard in Rome, a man named Vitalianus. Gordian knew that the prefect committed the most savage and cruel acts and that he was an intimate and devoted friend of Maximinus. Gordian suspected that Vitalianus would strenuously resist what he was trying to do, and he further suspected that the Romans' fear of the prefect would keep them from assisting him. Consequently, he sent to Rome the quaestor of the province, a bold and physically powerful man who, in the prime of youth, was eager to risk any danger for his emperor. Gordian assigned several centurions and a contingent of soldiers to the quaestor and gave him sealed dispatches written on the folding tablets by which secret messages were sent to the emperors. He ordered these men to enter Rome before dawn and approach Vitalianus while he was still hearing cases, after he had withdrawn into the little office in the courtroom where, alone, he opened and read the private messages which seemed to bear upon the emperor's safety. Gordian further told them to inform the prefect that they were carrying secret messages which con-

BOOK SEVEN

7 cerned Maximinus and that he had sent them on a matter involving the emperor's safety. He ordered these men to pretend that they wished to speak with Vitalianus privately and deliver their report; while he was examining the seals on the dispatches, they were to ask him some question and kill him with the swords concealed beneath their robes. It all happened precisely as Gordian had ordered. Since Vitalianus was accustomed to appear before daybreak, the messengers came to him privately while it was still dark and only a few people
8 were with him. Some visitors had not yet arrived; others had greeted him before dawn and had already left. All was quiet, with only a few people outside his door. When the messengers from Gordian revealed to the prefect what has been described above, they were readily admitted. Handing him the dispatches, they drew their daggers while he was examining the seals and stabbed him to death; then, holding their daggers ready for action, they sprang from the house.
9 Those who were present drew back in astonishment, thinking that Maximinus had ordered the murder, for he often did this sort of thing even to those who seemed to be his most intimate friends. Hurrying down the Sacred Way, the assassins displayed the letters of Gordian to the people and handed over his directives to the consuls and other officials. And now the rumor spread that Maximinus had been assassinated.

CHAPTER VII

WHEN these reports became known, the people milled about as if possessed. The fact is that all peoples are eager for a change of government, but the Roman mob, because of its tremendous size and diverse elements, is un-
2 usually prone to instability and vacillation. Therefore the statues, paintings, and all of Maximinus' emblems of honor were destroyed, and the hatred which fear had hitherto sup-

MAXIMINUS AND THE GORDIANS

pressed now poured forth without hindrance, freely and fearlessly. The senators met before they received accurate information concerning Maximinus and, placing their trust for the future in the present situation, proclaimed Gordian Augustus, together with his son, and destroyed Maximinus' emblems of honor. Informers and men who were bringing lawsuits either fled or were killed by those against whom they had brought unjust charges; officials and judges who had been the instruments of his savagery were dragged about the city by the mob and were then thrown into the sewers. There was great slaughter of those innocent of wrongdoing: without warning, men broke into the houses of their creditors and their opponents in lawsuits, indeed into the house of anyone they hated for some trivial reason; after threatening and abusing them as informers, their attackers robbed and killed them. Acts of civil war were committed in the name of freedom and peace and security; for example, the man who had been appointed prefect of the city after having held many consular offices (his name was Sabinus) was struck on the head by a stone and killed while he was trying to prevent what was happening in the city.

This is what the people did, but the senate, once it recognized the danger, did everything in its power to induce the provinces to revolt against Maximinus. Embassies composed of senators and distinguished Equestrians were sent to all the governors with letters which clearly revealed the attitude of the senate and the Roman people. These letters requested the governors to aid the common fatherland and the senate with their counsel, and urged the provinces to remain loyal to Rome, where the power and authority from the beginning had been in the hands of the people, whose friends and subjects the provinces were from the time of their ancestors. The majority of the governors welcomed the embassies and had no difficulty in arousing the provinces to revolt because

BOOK SEVEN

of the general hatred of Maximinus. After killing the provincial officials who favored Maximinus, the governors came to the support of the Romans. A few of the governors, however, killed the envoys who came to them or sent them to Maximinus under guard; these, upon their arrival, he tortured to death in savage fashion.

CHAPTER VIII

THIS was the situation with respect to the city and the attitude of the Romans. When these events were reported to Maximinus, he was enraged, but, although he was seriously concerned, he pretended to ignore the matter. On the first and second days he remained quietly in his headquarters, consulting with his friends about a plan of action. The whole army there with him and all the civilians in that region knew of the developments at Rome, and were amazed at the spirit of bold insubordination revealed by these acts; no one talked about the affair, however, each man pretending to be ignorant of what was occurring. So great was Maximinus' apprehension that he allowed nothing to escape his notice; he kept close watch on all, concerned not only with what they said but even with their facial expressions. Then, summoning the entire army to the plain in front of the city, the emperor came forth on the third day, carrying the speech which some of his friends had written for him:[1]

"I know that what I am going to say to you will sound strange and incredible, and I believe that you will find my remarks ridiculous and amusing, rather than awe-inspiring. It is not the Germans who are taking up arms to oppose you and your valor, those men whom we have conquered so often, nor the Sarmatians, who daily plead with us for peace. The Persians, who not long ago were overrunning Mesopo-

---
[1] A nice touch, to account for the elegant speech of the nonliterary emperor.

MAXIMINUS AND THE GORDIANS

tamia, are now subdued, happy to enjoy what they have, kept in check by the repute of your great skill in arms, and by the trial which they made of my military talents, of which they got a thorough knowledge when I commanded the armies on the riverbank. But the fact is (and you will have to laugh when you hear it) that the Carthaginians have taken leave of their senses and have either persuaded or compelled a miserable old man, doddering in advanced senility, to accept the throne, making sport of the empire as if in deliberate mockery. In what army do they trust, these men among whom lictors are sufficient to protect the proconsul? What kind of weapons do they carry, these men who have no arms except the spears they use in single combat with animals? Dancing, sarcastic quips, and rhythmic posturing are their methods of training for war. Let no one be frightened by the report of what has happened at Rome. Taken unaware by deceit and treachery, Vitalianus was murdered, but you know the unstable and capricious nature of the Roman mob, and you know that it is bold only as long as nothing is involved except shouting. But if that rabble sees only two or three armed men of the legions, each person is terrified at the thought of his own individual danger. Crowding together and trampling their neighbors, the rabble are indifferent to the common danger. If anyone has informed you of the senate's action, do not be surprised if our mild way of life seems irksome to the people and they prefer the undisciplined activities of Gordian; and do not wonder that they call manly and moderate acts fear-inspiring, and believe that unrestrained frenzy is civilized because it provides pleasure. They are, as a result, unfavorably disposed toward my rule because it is disciplined and well ordered, but they are delighted to hear the name of Gordian, whose reprehensible way of life is not unknown to you. It is with these and men like them that you will wage war, if anyone is willing to dignify it by that name. I believe that the majority, indeed, nearly everyone, will extend olive branches and hold out their children to us as soon as we set foot in Italy. They will throw themselves prostrate at our feet, while the rest will flee, in fear and trembling, and all their property will fall into my hands for distribution to you, and it will be your privilege to receive it and enjoy it in security."

9 After speaking thus, Maximinus attacked the senate and the Roman people with incoherent abuse, threatening gestures, and savage grimaces, as if he were enraged at his audience; he then publicly announced his departure for Rome. He made a lavish distribution of money to the soldiers, and delayed only a single day before beginning his march at the head of a huge force which included all the Roman armies.
10 A not inconsiderable force of Germans followed him; these he had either conquered by arms or had persuaded to join him in friendly alliance. He had engines of war and military machines, in fact everything he ordinarily took with him when he marched against the barbarians, and he slowed his progress further by collecting supplies and wagons from all
11 sides. As his journey to Rome was sudden and unexpected —not the usual sort but the result of hasty action—he gathered together whatever the army needed. He thought it best, under the circumstances, to send the Pannonians ahead; he had special confidence in these troops who had been first to proclaim him emperor and who wished and promised to risk their lives on his behalf. He ordered these soldiers to precede the rest of his force and seize the regions of Italy before his arrival.

CHAPTER IX

SO THE troops with Maximinus continued their march. Meanwhile, in Carthage, his affairs had prospered in a way he had not anticipated. A man of senatorial rank named

MAXIMINUS AND THE GORDIANS

Capelianus was at that time governor of the Moroccans under Roman rule, the ones called Numidians. This province was defended by garrison camps so located as to prevent marauding raids by the large number of Moroccan barbarians surrounding it. Capelianus thus had a formidable military force under his command. Gordian was hostile to Capelianus because they had earlier been involved in a lawsuit. When he assumed the title of emperor, Gordian sent a man to replace Capelianus and ordered the governor to leave the province. Angered by this, and devoted to Maximinus, who had appointed him governor, Capelianus assembled his entire army. Persuading his troops to remain loyal to Maximinus and faithful to their oath, the governor marched toward Carthage at the head of a huge army of young, vigorous men equipped with every type of weapon and trained for battle by military experience gained in fighting the barbarians.

When the report of this army's approach reached the city, Gordian was terrified; the Carthaginians, however, aroused by the news and thinking that their hope of victory lay in the size of a mob rather than in the discipline of an army, went forth in a body to oppose Capelianus. Then the elder Gordian, some say, was in despair because Capelianus was attacking Carthage; when he considered the size of Maximinus' army and reflected that there were no forces in Africa strong enough to match it, he hanged himself. His death was kept secret, however, and his son was chosen to command the crowd of civilians. When the battle was joined, the Carthaginians were superior in numbers, but they were an undisciplined mob, without military training; for they had grown up in a time of complete peace and indulged themselves constantly in feasts and festivals. To make it worse, they were without arms and proper equipment. Each man brought from home a dagger, an ax, or a hunting spear; those who found hides cut out circles of leather, arranged

BOOK SEVEN

pieces of wood as a frame, and fashioned shields as best they could. The Numidians, by contrast, were excellent javelin men and superb horsemen. Scorning a bridle they used only 7 a stick to guide their mounts. They easily routed the huge Carthaginian mob; without waiting for the Numidians' charge, the Carthaginians threw down their arms and fled. Crowding and trampling one another underfoot, more Carthaginians were killed in the crush than fell by enemy action. There the son of Gordian died, together with all his companions, and the number of dead was so great that it was impossible to gather them for burial. The body of the 8 young Gordian was never found. A few of the many who rushed into Carthage and found a place to hide managed to save themselves; they scattered throughout the city, which is huge and densely populated. The rest of the mob crowded before the gates of the city, trying to force their way in; attacked by the cavalry and legionary troops, they were cut 9 down to the last man. Loud wailing of women and children was heard everywhere in the city when they saw their loved ones slaughtered before their eyes. Others say that when these events were reported to the elder Gordian, who had remained behind because of his advanced age, and he was informed that Capelianus was marching into Carthage, in complete despair he went into his bedroom alone as if to rest; there he used the sash from his waist to hang himself.
10 Such was the fate of Gordian, whose life in the beginning was favored by Fortune and who died at least presenting the appearance of an emperor. When Capelianus entered Carthage, he put to death all the prominent men who survived the battle, plundered the temples, and seized the public and 11 private funds. Continuing to the rest of the cities which had destroyed Maximinus' emblems of honor, Capelianus killed the most important men, exiling the rest. He turned the farms and villages over to the soldiers to plunder and burn, pre-

MAXIMINUS AND THE GORDIANS

tending to be avenging Maximinus; the truth was, however, that he was scheming to win the good will of the soldiers so that if Maximinus should be killed he would have a loyal army and might thus lay claim to the empire.

CHAPTER X

THIS is what was happening in Africa. When the death of the elder Gordian was reported at Rome, the people and the senate particularly were completely bewildered, dumfounded to learn that Gordian, in whom they had placed their hope, was dead. They knew that Maximinus, who was naturally hostile and antagonistic toward them, would spare no one. Now that he had good reason for hatred, he would as a matter of course vent his rage upon them as upon acknowledged enemies. The senate therefore thought it best 2 to meet and consider what should be done. Since they had already cast the die, they voted to issue a declaration of war and choose two men from their own ranks to be joint emperors, dividing the imperial authority so that the power might not be in one man's hands and thus plunge them again into autocracy. They did not meet as usual in the senate house but in the temple of Jupiter Capitolinus, the god whom the Romans worship on the Capitoline Hill. They shut them- 3 selves up alone in this temple, as if to have Jupiter as their witness, fellow council member, and overseer of their actions. Choosing the men most distinguished for their age and merit, they approved them by ballot. Other senators received votes, but on the final count Maximus and Balbinus were elected joint emperors by majority opinion. Maximus had held many 4 army commands; appointed prefect of Rome, he administered the office with diligence and enjoyed among the people a good reputation for his understanding nature, his intelligence, and his moderate way of life. Balbinus, an aristocrat

BOOK SEVEN

who had twice served as consul and had governed provinces without complaint, had a more open and frank nature. After their election, the two men were proclaimed Augusti, and the senate awarded them by decree all the imperial honors.

While these actions were being taken on the Capitoline Hill, the people, whether they were informed by Gordian's friends and fellow countrymen or whether they learned it by rumor, filled the entire street leading up to the Capitol. The huge mob was armed with stones and clubs, for they objected to the senate's action and particularly disapproved of Maximus. The prefect ruled the city too strictly for the popular taste, and was very harsh in his dealings with the criminal and reckless elements of the mob. In their fear and dislike of Maximus, they kept shouting threats to kill both emperors, determined that the emperor be chosen from the family of Gordian and that the title remain in that house and under that name. Balbinus and Maximus surrounded themselves with an escort of swordsmen from the young Equestrians and the discharged soldiers living in Rome, and tried to force their way from the Capitol. The mob, armed with stones and clubs, prevented this until, at someone's suggestion, the people were deceived. There was in Rome at that time a little child, the son of Gordian's daughter, who bore his grandfather's name. The two emperors ordered some of their men to bring the child to the Capitol. Finding the lad playing at home, they lifted him to their shoulders and brought him to the Capitol through the midst of the crowd. Showing the boy to the people and telling them that he was the son of Gordian, they called him "Gordian," while the mob cheered the boy and scattered leaves in his path. The senate appointed him Caesar, since he was not old enough to be emperor. The mob, placated, allowed the imperial party to proceed to the palace.

CHAPTER XI

AT THIS same time a fatal blunder was made in Rome, one which originated in the rashness of two senators. The people of Rome were in the habit of coming to the senate house to find out what the senate was doing. When the praetorians whom Maximinus had left behind in the camp at Rome learned of this practice (they were discharged veterans who had remained at home because of their age), they came unarmed and in civilian dress to the door of the senate house to find out what was happening and stood there with the rest of the crowd. The other spectators remained outside, but two or three praetorians who were more curious than the rest, wishing to hear what was being planned, entered the council chamber, pushing past the base of the statue of Victory. Then a senator of the Carthaginian race named Gallicanus, who had recently been consul, and another senator named Maecenas, a man of praetorian rank, attacked the soldiers as they stood with their hands under their cloaks, and stabbed them to the heart with daggers hidden under their robes. As a result of the recent revolt and disorder, all the senators were armed with daggers, openly or secretly, claiming that they were carrying them for protection against possible enemy plots. The praetorians who were struck down on this occasion, having no opportunity to defend themselves because the attack was wholly unexpected, lay dead at the base of the statue of Victory. When the other praetorians saw this, they were terrified by the fate of their comrades. Unarmed and fearing the size of the mob, they turned and fled. Gallicanus ran out of the senate house into the crowd, displaying the dagger in his bloody hand, and ordered the mob to pursue and kill the enemies of the senate and the Roman people, the friends and support-

BOOK SEVEN

6 ers of Maximinus. The mob, easily persuaded, cheered Gallicanus and set out after the praetorians, hurling stones. The soldiers, few in number and wounded as well, fled before their pursuers; running into the praetorian camp, they shut the gates, took up arms, and posted guards on the walls. Gallicanus, by his reckless crime, brought civil war and
7 widespread destruction upon the city. He persuaded the people to break into the public arsenals, where armor used in parades rather than in battle was stored, each man to protect himself as best he could. He then threw open the gladiatorial schools and led out the gladiators armed with their regular weapons; finally, he collected all the spears, swords,
8 and axes from the houses and shops. The people, as if possessed, seized any tools they could find, made of suitable material, and fashioned weapons. They assembled and went out to the praetorian camp, where they attacked the gates and walls as if they were actually organizing a siege. The praetorians, with their vast combat experience, protected themselves behind their shields and the battlements; wounding their attackers with arrows and long spears, they kept
9 them from the walls and drove them back. With evening approaching, the besiegers decided to retire, since the civilians were exhausted and most of the gladiators were wounded. The people retreated in disorder, thinking that the few praetorians would not dare to pursue so large a mob. But the praetorians now threw open the gates and gave chase. They slaughtered the gladiators, and the greater part of the mob also perished, crushed in the confusion. After following the mob for a short distance, the praetorians returned and remained inside the walls of the camp.

CHAPTER XII

THIS debacle increased the fury of the mob and the senate. Generals were chosen and picked men were called up for service from all parts of Italy. The young men were assembled and armed with whatever weapons were at hand. Maximus led most of these soldiers out to attack Maximinus; the rest remained behind to guard and defend the city. Daily attacks were launched against the walls of the praetorian camp, but these assaults accomplished nothing, as the soldiers put up a stout resistance from their higher position. Struck and wounded, the attackers suffered heavily in the fighting. Balbinus, who had remained in Rome, issued an edict in which he pleaded with the people to effect a truce and promised amnesty to the soldiers, offering them pardon for all their offenses. But he failed in his efforts to persuade either side: so huge a mob thought it disgraceful to be defied by a mere handful of men, and the praetorians were enraged to be suffering these barbaric indignities at the hands of Romans.

Finally, when the attacks on the walls made no progress, the generals decided that it would be good strategy to block off all the streams flowing into the praetorian camp and thus overcome the soldiers by cutting off their water supply. They therefore stopped the flow of water into the camp and diverted it into other channels, damming up the beds of the streams which flowed under the walls. Recognizing the danger, the despairing praetorians opened the gate and rushed forth to the attack. A sharp skirmish resulted and, when the mob fled, the guards pursued and drove them into all parts of the city. Bested in the hand-to-hand fighting, the people climbed to the housetops and rained down upon the praetorians tiles, stones, and clay pots. In this way they inflicted severe injuries upon the soldiers, who, being unfamiliar with

the houses, did not dare to climb after them, and, of course, the doors of the shops and houses were barred. The soldiers did, however, set fire to houses that had wooden balconies
6 (and there were many of this type in the city). Because a great number of houses were made chiefly of wood, the fire spread very rapidly and without a break throughout most of the city. Many men who lost their vast and magnificent properties, valuable for the large incomes they produced and for their expensive decorations, were reduced from wealth to
7 poverty. A great many people died in the fire, unable to escape because the exits had been blocked by the flames. All the property of the wealthy was looted when the criminal and worthless elements in the city joined with the soldiers in plundering. And the part of Rome destroyed by fire was greater in extent than the largest intact city in the empire.
8 This was the situation at Rome. In the meantime, having completed his march, Maximinus was poised on the borders of Italy; after offering sacrifices at all the boundary altars, he advanced into Italy, ordering the troops to march under arms in battle formation.
9 We have now described in detail the revolt in the province of Africa, the civil war in Rome, the actions of Maximinus, and his advance into Italy; the events which followed will be related in the succeeding book.

BOOK EIGHT

MAXIMUS AND BALBINUS

CHAPTER I

MAXIMINUS' actions after the death of Gordian and his advance into Italy have been described in the preceding book, together with the revolt in Africa and the dissension which arose at Rome between the praetorians and the people. Halting at the borders, Maximinus sent scouts ahead to find out whether any soldiers lay in ambush in the valleys, thickets, or mountain forests. Leading his army down into level country, Maximinus drew up the legions in a broad, shallow rectangle in order to occupy most of the plain; he placed all the heavy baggage, supplies, and wagons in the center of the formation and, taking command of the rear guard, followed with his troops. On each flank marched the squadrons of armed cavalry, the Moroccan javelin men, and the archers from the East. The emperor also brought along a large number of German auxiliaries; he assigned these to the van to bear the initial assaults of the enemy. These men are savage and bold in the opening phases of battle; and if any risk were involved, the barbarian Germans were readily expendable. When the troops had crossed the plain in good

BOOK EIGHT

order and strict discipline, they came to the first city in Italy, the one called Ema by the natives. Ema is situated on an elevated plateau at the foot of the Alps. From there advance guards and army scouts returned to report to Maximinus that the city was deserted. The inhabitants had fled in a body after setting fire to the doors of the temples and houses. As they had burned or carried off everything in the cities and
5 fields, no food was left for men or animals. Maximinus was gratified by the immediate flight of these Italians, and now anticipated that all the people of Italy would flee at his approach. But the army was by no means pleased to find itself suffering from famine at the very outset. Therefore, after spending the night at Ema, some in the city in houses already stripped of doors and everything else, others in the fields around the city, at sunrise they pressed on to the Alps. The Alps are very tall mountains which nature has erected as a defensive wall for Italy; rising high above the clouds, they extend a great distance and encompass Italy from the Tyr-
6 rhenian Sea on the west to the Ionian Sea on the east. The mountains are covered with limitless dense forests, and the passes are narrow because of the towering cliffs or rough, broken rocks. These narrow passes are man-made, fashioned with much labor by the ancient Italians. The army advanced through these gaps with great anxiety, expecting the heights to be occupied and the paths blocked against their passage. Judging by the nature of the region, they were justified in their apprehensions.

CHAPTER II

WHEN no opposition was offered, they crossed the Alps without hindrance; coming down to level country, they grew bolder and sang songs of thanksgiving. As the Italians had not taken advantage of the rough terrain to hide and protect themselves, Maximinus expected everything to turn out successfully for him without the slightest difficulty. The Italians had not launched treacherous attacks from ambush or fought from the heights, taking advantage of the superior position. While the army was in the plain, the scouts reported that Aquileia, the largest city in that part of Italy, had closed its gates and that the Pannonian legions which had been sent ahead had launched a vigorous attack upon the walls of this city. In spite of frequent assaults, they were completely unsuccessful. Finally, showered with stones, spears, and a rain of arrows, the Pannonians gave up and withdrew. Enraged at the Pannonian generals for fighting too feebly, Maximinus hurried to the city with his army, expecting to capture it with no difficulty.

Before these events occurred, Aquileia was already a huge city, with a large permanent population. Situated on the sea and with all the provinces of Illyricum behind it, Aquileia served as a port of entry for Italy. The city thus made it possible for goods transported from the interior by land or by the rivers to be traded to the merchant mariners and also for the necessities brought by sea to the mainland, goods not produced there because of the cold climate, to be sent to the upland areas. Since the inland people farm a region that produces much wine, they export this in quantity to those who do not cultivate grapes. A huge number of people lived permanently in Aquileia, not only the native residents but also foreigners and merchants. At this time the city was even more crowded than usual; all the people from the surrounding area had left the small towns and villages and sought refuge there. They put their hope of safety in the city's great size and its defensive wall; this ancient wall, however, had for the most part collapsed. Under Roman rule the cities of Italy no longer had need of walls or arms; they had substituted permanent peace for war and had also gained a partici-

BOOK EIGHT

5 pating share in the Roman government. Now, however, necessity forced the Aquileians to repair the wall, rebuild the fallen sections, and erect towers and battlements. After fortifying the city with a rampart as quickly as possible, they closed the gates and remained together on the wall day and night, beating off their assailants. Two senators named Crispinus and Meniphilus, former consuls, were appointed gener-
6 als. These two had seen to everything with careful attention. With great foresight they had brought into the city supplies of every kind in quantities sufficient to enable it to withstand a long siege. An ample supply of water was available from the many wells in the city, and, a river flowing at the foot of the city wall provided both a defensive moat and an abundance of water.

CHAPTER III

THESE are the preparations which had been made in the city. When it was reported to Maximinus that Aquileia was well defended and tightly shut, he thought it wise to send envoys to discuss the situation with the townspeople from the foot of the wall and try to persuade them to open the gates. There was in the besieging army a tribune who was a native of Aquileia, and whose wife, children, and rela-
2 tives were inside the city. Maximinus sent this man to the wall accompanied by several centurions, expecting their fellow citizen to win them over easily. The envoys told the Aquileians that Maximinus, their mutual emperor, ordered them to lay down their arms in peace, to receive him as a friend, not as an enemy, and to turn from killing to libations and sacrifices. Their emperor directed them not to overlook the fact that their native city was in danger of being razed to its very foundations, whereas it was in their power to save themselves and to preserve their city when their merciful em-

peror pardoned them for their offenses. Others, not they, were the guilty ones. The envoys shouted their message from the foot of the wall so that those above might understand it. Most of the city's population was on the walls and in the towers; only those standing guard at other posts were absent. They all listened quietly to what the envoys were saying. Fearing that the people, convinced by these lying promises, might choose peace instead of war and throw open the gates, Crispinus ran along the parapet, pleading with the Aquileians to hold out bravely and offer stout resistance; he begged them not to break faith with the senate and the Roman people, but to win a place in history as the saviors and defenders of all Italy. He warned them not to trust the promises of a tyrant, a liar, and a hypocrite, and not to surrender to certain destruction, lulled by soft words, when they could put their trust in the always unpredictable outcome of war. Often, he continued, few have prevailed over many and those who appeared to be weaker have overcome those assumed to be stronger. Nor should they be frightened by the size of the besieging army. "Those who fight on another's behalf," he said, "well aware that the benefits, if any should result, will be not theirs but his, are less eager to do battle, knowing that while they share the risks, another will reap the greatest prizes of the victory. But those who fight for their native land can look for greater favor from the gods because they do not pray for help in seizing the property of others, but ask only to be allowed to retain in safety what is already theirs. They show an enthusiasm for battle which results not from the orders of another but from their own inner compulsion, since all the fruits of victory belong to them and them alone." By saying such things as these, Crispinus, who was venerable by nature and highly skilled in speaking Latin, and had governed the Aquileians moderately, succeeded in persuading them to remain at their assigned posts; he ordered the envoys

BOOK EIGHT

to return unsuccessful to Maximinus. He is said to have persevered in his prosecution of the war because the many men in the city who were skilled at auguries and the taking of auspices reported that the omens favored the townspeople. The Italians place particular reliance upon the taking of auguries. Oracles, too, revealed to them that their native god promised them victory. They call this god Belis, and worship him with special devotion, identifying him with Apollo, whose image, some of Maximinus' soldiers said, often appeared in the sky over the city, fighting for the Aquileians. Whether the god actually appeared to some of the besiegers, or whether they simply said that he did because they were ashamed that so large an army was unable to overcome a mob of civilians, and it would thus seem that they had been beaten by gods, not by men, I am unable to say, but the strangeness of the whole affair makes everything about it credible.

CHAPTER IV

WHEN the envoys returned unsuccessful, Maximinus, in a towering rage, pressed on toward the city with increased speed. But when he came to a large river sixteen miles from Aquileia, he found it flowing very wide and very deep. The warmth at that season of the year had melted the mountain snow that had been frozen all winter, and a vast, snow-swollen flood had resulted. It was impossible for Maximinus' army to cross this river because the Aquileians had destroyed the bridge, a huge structure of imposing proportions built, by earlier emperors, of squared stones and supported on tapering piers. Since neither bridges nor boats were available, the army halted in confusion. Some of the Germans, unfamiliar with the swift, violent rivers of Italy and thinking that these flowed down to the plains as lazily as their own streams (it is the slow current of the German rivers which causes them to freeze over), entered the river with their horses, which are trained to swim, and were carried away and drowned.

After a ditch had been dug around the camp to prevent attacks, Maximinus halted for two or three days beside the river, considering how it might be bridged. Timber was scarce, and there were no boats which could be fastened together to span the river. Some of his engineers, however, called attention to the many empty wooden kegs scattered about the deserted fields, the barrels which the natives use to ship wine safely to those forced to import it. The kegs are hollow, like boats; when fastened together and anchored to the shore by cables, they float like pontoons, and the current cannot carry them off. Planks are laid on top of these pontoons, and with great skill and speed a bank of earth is piled up evenly on the platform thus fashioned. After the bridge had been completed, the army crossed over and marched to Aquileia, where they found the buildings on the outskirts deserted. The soldiers cut down all the trees and grapevines and burned them, and destroyed the crops which had already begun to appear in those regions. Since the trees were planted in even rows and the interwoven vines linked them together everywhere, the countryside had a festive air; one might even say that it wore a garland of green. All these trees and vines Maximinus' soldiers cut down to the very roots before they hurried up to the walls of Aquileia. The army was exhausted, however, and it seemed wiser not to launch an immediate attack. The soldiers therefore remained out of range of the arrows and took up stations around the entire circuit of the wall by cohorts and legions, each unit investing the section it was ordered to hold. After a single day's rest, the soldiers kept the city under continuous siege for the remaining time.

They brought up every type of siege machinery and at-

BOOK EIGHT

7 tacked the wall with all the power they could muster, leaving untried nothing of the art of siege warfare. They launched numerous assaults virtually every day, and the entire army held the city encircled as if in a net, but the Aquileians fought back determinedly, showing real enthusiasm for war. They had closed their houses and temples and were fighting in a body, together with the women and children, from their advantageous position on the parapet and in the towers. In this way they held off their attackers, and no one was too young or too old to take part in the battle to preserve his native city.

8 All the buildings in the suburbs and outside the city gates were demolished by Maximinus' men, and the wood from the houses was used to build the siege engines. The soldiers made every effort to destroy a part of the wall, so that the army might break in, seize everything, and, after leveling the city, leave the area a deserted pasture land. The journey to Rome would not be fittingly glorious if Maximinus failed

9 to capture the first city in Italy to oppose him. By pleading and promising gifts, Maximinus and his son, whom he had appointed his Caesar, spurred the army to action; they rode about on horseback, encouraging the soldiers to fight with resolution. The Aquileians hurled down stones on the besiegers; combining pitch and olive oil with asphalt and brimstone, they ignited this mixture and poured it over their attackers from hollow vessels fitted with long handles. Bringing the flaming liquid to the walls, they scattered it over the

10 soldiers like a heavy downpour of rain. Carried along with the other ingredients, the pitch oozed onto the unprotected parts of the soldiers' bodies and spread everywhere. Then the soldiers ripped off their blazing corselets and the rest of their armor too, for the iron grew red hot, and the leather and wooden parts caught fire and burned. As a result, soldiers were seen everywhere stripping themselves, and the discarded armor appeared like the spoils of war, but these were

MAXIMUS AND BALBINUS

taken by cunning and treachery, not by courage on the field of battle. In this tragedy, most of the soldiers suffered scarred and disfigured faces and lost eyes and hands, while every unprotected part of the body was severely injured. The Aquileians hurled down torches on the siege engines which had been dragged up to the walls. These torches, sharpened at the end like a javelin, were soaked in pitch and resin and then ignited; the firebrands, still blazing, stuck fast in the machines, which easily caught fire and were consumed by the flames.

CHAPTER V

DURING the opening days, then, the fortunes of war were almost equal. As time passed, however, the army of Maximinus grew depressed and, cheated in its expectations, fell into despair when the soldiers found that those whom they had not expected to hold out against a single assault were not only offering stout resistance but were even beating them back. The Aquileians, on the other hand, were greatly encouraged and highly enthusiastic, and, as the battle continued, their skill and daring increased. Contemptuous of the soldiers now, they hurled taunts at them. As Maximinus rode about, they shouted insults and indecent blasphemies at him and his son. The emperor became increasingly angry because he was powerless to retaliate. Unable to vent his wrath upon the enemy, he was enraged at most of his troop commanders because they were pressing the siege in cowardly and halfhearted fashion. Consequently, the hatred of his supporters increased, and his enemies grew more contemptuous of him each day.

As it happened, the Aquileians had everything they needed in abundant quantities. With great foresight they had stored in the city all the food and drink required for men and ani-

BOOK EIGHT

mals. The soldiers of the emperor, by contrast, lacked every necessity, since they had cut down the fruit trees and devastated the countryside. Some of the soldiers had built temporary huts, but the majority were living in the open air, exposed to sun and rain. And now many died of starvation; no food was brought in from the outside, as the Romans had blocked all the roads of Italy by erecting walls provided with narrow gates. The senate dispatched former consuls and picked men from all Italy to guard the beaches and harbors and prevent anyone from sailing. Their intent was to keep Maximinus in ignorance of what was happening at Rome; thus the main roads and all the bypaths were closely watched to prevent anyone's passing. The result was that the army which appeared to be maintaining the siege was itself under siege, for it was unable to capture Aquileia or leave the city and proceed to Rome; all the boats and wagons had been hidden, and no vehicles of any kind were available to the soldiers. Exaggerated rumors were circulated, based only on suspicion, to the effect that the entire Roman people were under arms; that all Italy was united; that the provinces of Illyricum and the barbarian nations in the East and South had gathered an army; and that everywhere men were solidly united in hatred of Maximinus. The emperor's soldiers were in despair and in need of everything. There was scarcely even sufficient water for them. The only source of water was the nearby river, which was fouled by blood and bodies. Lacking any means of burying those who died in the city, the Aquileians threw the bodies into the river; both those who fell in the fighting and those who died of disease were dropped into the stream, as the city had no facilities for burial.

And so the completely confused army was in the depths of despair. Then one day, during a lull in the fighting, when most of the soldiers had gone to their quarters or their stations, Maximinus was resting in his tent. Without warning,

MAXIMUS AND BALBINUS

the soldiers whose camp was near Rome at the foot of Mount Alba,[1] where they had left their wives and children, decided that the best solution was to kill Maximinus and end the interminable siege. They resolved no longer to ravage Italy for an emperor they now knew to be a despicable tyrant. Taking courage, therefore, the conspirators went to Maximinus' tent about noon. The imperial bodyguard, which was involved in the plot, ripped Maximinus' pictures from the standards; when he came out of his tent with his son to talk to them, they refused to listen and killed them both [A.D. 238]. They killed the army's commanding general also, and the emperor's close friends. Their bodies were handed over to those who wished to trample and mutilate them, after which the corpses were exposed to the birds and dogs. The heads of Maximinus and his son were sent to Rome. Such was the fate suffered by Maximinus and his son, who paid the penalty for their savage rule.

CHAPTER VI

WHEN the soldiers were informed of what had happened, they were to a man dumfounded, but by no means all the troops were pleased about the assassination. The Pannonians and the barbarians from Thrace were especially angered, for these were the men who had actually placed the empire in Maximinus' hands. Since the deed was accomplished, they tolerated it, but unwillingly; they had no choice but to be hypocritical and pretend to be pleased with all that had happened. Then, laying down their arms, the soldiers came to the walls of Aquileia, this time in peace, and reported the assassination of Maximinus, expecting the Aquileians to throw open the gates and welcome as friends yesterday's enemies. The Aquileian generals, however, did not

---
[1] *Legio II Parthica,* stationed near Rome by Severus to protect the city.

BOOK EIGHT

allow the gates to be opened to them; bringing forward the statues of Maximus and Balbinus and Gordian Caesar, they cheered these rulers themselves and thought it appropriate that Maximinus' soldiers also acknowledge them and shout their approval of the emperors chosen by the senate and the
3 Roman people. They informed the soldiers that the other two Gordians had gone to join Jupiter in heaven. And now the Aquileians set up a market on the walls, offering for sale a huge quantity of goods of all kinds, including ample supplies of food, drink, clothing, and shoes—in short, everything that a prosperous and flourishing city could provide for human
4 consumption. At this the soldiers were even more amazed; they now realized that the Aquileians had enough of everything they needed even if the siege were prolonged, whereas they lacked all the necessities and would have perished to the last man before they captured a city so abundantly supplied. The army continued to remain in position around the city, while the soldiers purchased what they needed from the walls, each man buying as much as he chose. In the meantime, they discussed the situation among themselves. A state of peace and amity actually existed, even though the surrounded city appeared still under siege, with the army encamped on all sides.
5 This was the situation at Aquileia. The horsemen carrying the head of Maximinus to Rome made the journey at top speed; the gates of all the cities on their route were thrown open to receive them, and the people welcomed them with laurel branches. When they had crossed the marshes and shallows between Altinum and Ravenna, they found the emperor Maximus in Ravenna levying picked men from
6 Rome and Italy. The Germans sent to Maximus a large number of auxiliary troops; their good will toward the man was of long standing and resulted from his moderate governorship of their country. While he was preparing for war against

MAXIMUS AND BALBINUS

Maximinus, the horsemen arrived with the heads of the emperor and his son and reported the victory. They informed Maximus that the army was in agreement with the Romans about the emperors and had sworn allegiance to the men elected by the senate. When these unexpected developments were announced, sacrifices were led to the altars, and all joined in celebrating a victory won without striking a blow. Finding the omens favorable, Maximus sent the horsemen on to Rome to report to the people what had happened and to display the heads of the two men. When the messengers arrived, they rushed into the city and raised on high the heads of their enemies impaled on a spear for all to see. No words can describe the rejoicing in the city on that day. Men of all ages rushed headlong to the altars and temples; no one remained at home, but, like men possessed, the people congratulated each other and poured into the Circus Maximus as if a public assembly were being held there. Balbinus sacrificed a hecatomb, and all the magistrates and the entire senate shouted with joy, each feeling that he had escaped an ax suspended over his head. Messengers and heralds with laurel branches were sent around to the provinces.

CHAPTER VII

THUS was holiday kept at Rome. Meanwhile, Maximus left Ravenna and proceeded to Aquileia, crossing on his way the shallows fed by the Eridanus River and the surrounding marshes; these shallows empty into the sea through seven outlets, and for this reason the natives call the marsh, in their own language, the "Seven Seas." The Aquileians immediately opened their gates and welcomed Maximus into the city. Now all the cities of Italy sent embassies to him of their most distinguished citizens, clad in white and carrying laurel branches. Each group brought the statues of its ances-

BOOK EIGHT

tral gods and the gold crowns among the votive offerings. These men cheered Maximus and scattered leaves in his path. The soldiers who were besieging Aquileia now came forward, carrying the laurel branches symbolic of peaceful intent, not because this represented their true feelings but because the presence of the emperor forced them to pretend

3 respect and good will. The truth is that most of the soldiers were secretly angered and grieved to see their chosen emperor killed and the emperors elected by the senate in full command. In Aquileia, Maximus attended to the sacrifices on the first and second days; on the third day, however, he summoned the entire army to the plain and from a platform erected for his use addressed them as follows:

4 "How much it has profited you to change your minds and support the actions of the Romans you have learned from recent experience. Now you are at peace instead of at war. You are enjoying the protection of the gods by whom you swore. And you are keeping your soldier's oath, that sacred rite of the Roman empire. All good things are yours to enjoy from this time on, for you have confirmed your pledges to the senate and the Roman people and to us, your emperors, chosen by the senate and the people for our nobility of birth, the many positions of authority we have held, and the long succession of offices which made it appear that we had risen

5 to the throne by a regular *cursus*. The empire is the personal property of no man. It is from of old the common possession of the people of Rome, the seat of your empire's fortune. To us and to you have been entrusted the administration and management of that empire. With good discipline and proper behavior, with respect and honor for those who command you, a prosperous life, full of every good thing, will be yours. For all other men in the provinces and the cities, peace will result, and obedience to their governors. You will be able to live as you like among your kinsmen; you will not suffer

injury in some foreign land. As to the matter of keeping the barbarian nations quiet, that will be our concern. As two emperors invested with equal power, we shall manage affairs at Rome jointly. Should any difficulty arise abroad, one of us can easily be present wherever and whenever the occasion demands. Let no one of you think that we shall remember what has occurred, either what you did (for you were simply obeying orders) or what the Romans and the other provincials did, for they rebelled because they were unjustly treated. But rather let us proclaim an amnesty for all offenses, and let there be pacts of lasting friendship and pledges of eternal good will and good conduct."

After this speech, Maximus promised the soldiers lavish gifts of money; then, remaining in Aquileia only a few days longer, he arranged to return to Rome. He sent the rest of the army to the provinces and to duty in their own local garrisons, while he went to Rome with the praetorians, the guards of the imperial palace, and the troops enrolled by Balbinus. The auxiliaries from Germany also accompanied him to Rome; he put great faith in their loyalty, relying on the fact that before he became emperor he had governed the province of Germany in moderate fashion. Balbinus came out to meet his co-emperor on the outskirts of Rome, bringing with him Gordian Caesar. The senate and the people welcomed Maximus with cheers, as if he were celebrating a triumph.

CHAPTER VIII

FOR the rest of the time the two emperors governed in an orderly and well-regulated manner, winning approval on every hand both privately and publicly. The people honored and respected them as patriotic and admirable rulers of the empire. The praetorians, however, were privately disgruntled, not at all pleased that the people had demonstrated

BOOK EIGHT

their approval of the emperors. The noble birth of the two men was an affront to the praetorians, and they were indignant also because the emperors had received the imperial office from the senate. The praetorians feared that the German troops with Maximus in Rome would oppose them if they should instigate a revolt. They suspected that the Germans were lying in wait for them; if the praetorians were discharged from service by trickery, the Germans would be at hand to replace them as the imperial bodyguard. They recalled the example of Severus, who dismissed the praetorians who had killed Pertinax.

When the Capitoline Games were drawing to an end and all the people were occupied with festivals and shows, the praetorians suddenly brought their hidden resentments into the open. Making no attempt to control their anger, they launched an unreasoning assault; rushing into the palace with one purpose, they approached the aged emperors. It so happened that the two men were not in complete accord: so great is the desire for sole rule and so contrary to the usual practice is it for the sovereignty to be shared that each undertook to secure the imperial power for himself alone. Balbinus considered himself the more worthy because of his noble birth and his two terms as consul; Maximus felt that he deserved first place because he had served as prefect of Rome and had won a good reputation by his administrative efforts. Both men were led to covet the sole rule because of their distinguished birth, aristocratic lineage, and the size of their families. This rivalry was the basis of their downfall. When Maximus learned that the Praetorian Guard was coming to kill them, he wished to summon a sufficient number of the German auxiliaries who were in Rome to resist the conspirators. But Balbinus, thinking that this was a ruse intended to deceive him (he knew that the Germans were devoted to Maximus), refused to allow Maximus to issue the order, believing that the Germans were coming not to put down a

MAXIMUS AND BALBINUS

praetorian uprising but to secure the empire for Maximus alone. While the two men were arguing, the praetorians rushed in with a single purpose. When the guards at the palace gates deserted the emperors, the praetorians seized the old men and ripped off the plain robes they were wearing because they were at home. Dragging the two men naked from the palace, they inflicted every insult and indignity upon them. Jeering at these emperors elected by the senate, they beat and tortured them, pulling their beards and eyebrows and doing them every kind of physical outrage. They then brought the emperors through the middle of the city to the praetorian camp, unwilling to kill them in the palace; they preferred to torture them first, so that they might suffer longer. When the Germans learned what was happening, they snatched up their arms and hastened to the rescue. As soon as the praetorians were informed of their approach, they killed the mutilated emperors. Leaving the corpses exposed in the street, the praetorians took up Gordian Caesar and proclaimed him emperor, since at the moment they could find no other candidate for the office. Proclaiming that they had only killed the men whom the people did not want to rule them in the first place, they chose as emperor this Gordian who was descended from the Gordian whom the Romans themselves had forced to accept the rule. Keeping their emperor Gordian with them, they went off to the praetorian camp, where they shut the gates and remained quiet. Learning that the men they were hurrying to rescue had been killed and their bodies exposed, the Germans returned to their quarters, unwilling to fight fruitlessly for men already dead.

Such was the undeserved and impious fate suffered by these two respected and distinguished elder statesmen, nobly born men deservedly elevated to the imperial throne. Gordian, at the age of about thirteen, was designated emperor and assumed the burden of the Roman empire [A.D. 238].

INDEX

(References are to book, chapter, and section, in that order.)

Abgarus, III ix 2
Adventus: Caracalla's general, IV xii 1; chosen emperor, IV xiv 2
Aemilianus: Niger's general, defeated by Severus, III ii 2, 3; accused of betraying Niger, III ii 3
Aesculapius, IV viii 3
Africa: procurator slain, VII iv. *See also* Capelianus; Carthaginians; Moroccans.
Albinus, governor of Britain: appointed Caesar by Severus, II xv 1-6, III vii 8; Severus plots against, III v, vi 1-8; defeated by Severus, III vi 10, vii 1-7; killed, III vii 7; friends in Rome killed by Severus, III viii 1-2, 6
Alexander the Great, I iii 2, III iv 3, IV viii 1-3, 7, 9, ix 3, 4, V vii 3, VI ii 2, 6; generals of, IV viii 2; tomb of, IV viii 9
Alexandrians: character of, IV viii 6-9, ix 1-3
Alexianus. *See* Severus Alexander.
Aquileia: importance of, VIII ii 2-5; siege of, VIII ii 5-6, iii, iv, v; army surrenders to, VIII vi 2-4; welcomes Maximus, VIII vii 2-3
Armenia, king of, III i 2, ix 2
Arsaces, VI ii 7
Artabanus, king of Parthia: aids Niger, III i 2; routed by Severus, III ix 9-11; defeated by Caracalla, IV x, xi 1, 2, 5; expedition against Caracalla, IV xiv 1, 3-8, xv; killed by Artaxerxes, VI ii 1, 7, iii 5
Artaxerxes, king of Persia: threat to Roman Empire, VI ii, iii 5-6, iv 4-6; kills Artabanus, VI ii 1, 7, iii 5; defeats S. Alexander, VI v, vi 3; disbands army, VI vi 5
Atrenians: Severus marches against, III ix 2, 3; Hatra besieged, III ix 4-7. *See also* Barsemius.

Balbinus: proclaimed emperor with Maximus, VII x 3-5; character, VII x 4; appoints Gordian III Caesar, VII x 5-9; tries to end civil war in Rome, VII xii 2-3; informed of Maximinus' death, VIII vi 8; joint rule, VIII vii 8, viii 1; rivalry, VIII viii 4-5; killed by praetorians, VIII viii 5-8
Barsemius, king of Atrenians, III i 2, 3, v 1, ix 1
Bassianus. *See* Elagabalus.

INDEX

Britain: divided into two provinces, III viii 2; revolt of, III xiv. *See also* Albinus.

Britons: description of, III xiv 6–8

Byzantium: occupied by Niger, III i 5–7, ii 1; siege and capture, III vi 9; headquarters of Caracalla, IV iii 6

Camel troops, IV xv 2–3

Capelianus, governor of Africa: restores Africa to Maximinus, VII ix

Caracalla: married to daughter of Plautianus, III x 5; rejects wife, III x 8, xiii 2; rivalry with brother Geta, III x 3–4, xiii 2, xv 7, IV i 1–2, 5, iii 1, iv 1–2; removal of Plautianus, III xii 10–12; wife sent to Sicily by Severus, III xiii 3; battles in Britain, III xiv 9; plot to gain control of army fails, III xv 1, 5, 6; returns to Rome, III xv 7; character, IV iii 3–4; partition of empire proposed, IV iii 5–9; kills Geta, IV iv 2–3, v 4–5; proclaimed emperor, IV iv 8; speech to senate, IV v 2–7; kills wife, IV vi 3; in Danube area, identifies with German soldiers, IV vii 2–7; in Thrace, identifies with Alexander the Great, IV viii 1–3; in Pergamum and Troy, identifies with Achilles, IV viii 3–5; in Antioch, IV viii 6, ix 8; in Alexandria, IV viii 8–9; plot to massacre Alexandrian youth, IV ix; deceives Artabanus, IV x 1–4; routs Parthians through treachery, IV xi 4–7, xiv 1; in Mesopotamia, IV xi 8–9; consults diviners, IV xii 3–5; plot of Macrinus, IV xii 6–8, xv 6, 8; killed by Martialis, IV xiii 3–8; compared with Macrinus, V ii 5

Carthaginians: character of, VII viii 5–6; attacked by Capelianus, VII ix 4 ff.

Chalcedon: headquarters of Geta, IV iii 6

Cleander: rise to power under Commodus, I xii 3; plots to seize empire, I xii 3–4; killed by order of Commodus, I xiii 4, 6

Commodus: rearing, I ii 1–2; speech to army, I v 3–8; buys peace from Germans in order to return to Rome, I vi 8–9, vii 2–3, 6; ancestry, I vii 4, xvii 12, II x 3; appearance, I vii 5, xvii 12; marries Crispina, I viii 4; escapes plot of Lucilla and Quadratus, I viii 4–8; escapes plot of Perennis, I ix 1–10; appoints two praetorian prefects, I ix 10; plot of Maternus, I x; leaves Rome to escape plague, I xii 1–2; conspiracy of Cleander quelled, I xii 3–9, xiii 1–6; infamous deeds and irrational conduct, I xiii 7–8, xiv 7–9, xv 7–9; skill in marksmanship, I xv 1–6, xvii 12; killed as result of plot by Marcia, Eclectus, and Laetus, I xvi, xvii; Pertinax, II i 4

Crispina, I viii 4

Crispinus, VIII ii 5, iii 4–7

Deification: of Severus, IV ii; of Maesa, VI i 4; of Gordians, VIII vi 3

Eclectus: plot to kill Commodus, I xvi, xvii; selects Pertinax as emperor, II i 3–10

INDEX

Elagabalus (Bassianus): priest of sun god, V iii 4–9, v 3–10, vi 3–9; rumored to be son of Caracalla, V iii 10–12; proclaimed emperor, V iii 11–12; Macrinus defeated and killed, V iv 5–12; marital career, V vi 1–2; S. Alexander appointed Caesar, V vii 1–6; misrule, V vii 6–7; plots to remove S. Alexander, V viii 2–8; killed by praetorians, V viii 8–9
Elagabalus (sun god), V iii 4–6, v 3–4, 6–9, vi 3–9

Festus, IV viii 4–5

Gallicanus, VII xi 3–7
Games: Capitoline, I ix 2; Secular, III viii 10
Germanicus, cognomen of Commodus, I xv 9
Germans: threat of, I iii 5, VI vii 2–9; as bodyguards, IV vii 3, xiii 6; defeated by Maximinus, VII ii; as auxiliaries, VIII i 3, vi 6, viii 2
Geta: governs Britain in absence of Severus, III xiv 9; rivalry with brother Caracalla, III x 3–4, xiii 2, xv 7, IV i 1–2, 5, iii 1, iv 1–2; character, IV iii 2–3; partition of empire proposed, IV iii 5–9; killed by Caracalla, IV iv 2–3, v 4–5; associates killed, IV vi 1–4
Glabrionus, II iii 3–4
Gordian I, proconsul of Africa: hailed as emperor, VII v; given title of Africanus, VII v 8; has Vitalianus killed, VII vi 4–9; proclaimed emperor at Rome, VII vii 2; commits suicide as Capelianus' army approaches, VII ix 4, 9, x 1
Gordian II: proclaimed emperor with Gordian I, VII vii 2; killed in battle against Capelianus, VII ix 5–8
Gordian III: proclaimed Caesar, VII x 5–9; proclaimed emperor by praetorians, VIII viii 7–8
Greeks, character of, III ii 7–9

Herodian: concern with truth, I i 3–6; on Marcus Aurelius, I ii 5; on Severus, II ix 4, 6, xv 6–7

Illyricum: army of, I ix 1, 4, II viii 10, ix 1, 8, 9, x 1, 8, xi 7, 9, xiii 10, xiv 6, xv 5, III i 1, VI iv 3, vi 2, vii 3; provinces of, VI vii 2, 4, VIII ii 3, v 6

Julia, wife of Severus: tries to reconcile Caracalla and Geta, III xv 6, IV iii 4–9; dies at Antioch, IV xiii 8
Julianus: praetorian prefect under Macrinus, V iv 2–3; killed, V iv 4
Julianus, Didius: purchases empire after assassination of Pertinax, II vi 6–14; imperial activities, II vii 1–3; deserted by praetorians, II vii 6, viii 5; prepares to resist Severus, II xi 7–9, xii 1, 2; killed by order of senate, II xii 3–7, xiii 1, III vii 8

Laetus, praetorian prefect: plots to kill Commodus, I xvi, xvii; selects Pertinax as emperor, II i 3–10, ii 1–2

INDEX

Laetus, general of Severus, III vii 3–5

Lucilla, daughter of Marcus Aurelius: marries Lucius Verus, I viii 3; marries Pompeianus, I viii 3; plots against Commodus, I viii 4; killed by Commodus, I viii 8; son killed by Caracalla, IV vi 3

Macedon: kills Quartinus, VII i 10; killed by Maximinus, VII i 11

Macrinus: plots to remove Caracalla, IV xii, xiii; discovers plot of Materianus against him, IV xii 6–8; persuades Martialis to kill Caracalla, IV xiii; chosen emperor by army, IV xiv 2–3; speech to soldiers, IV xiv 4–8; battle with Artabanus, IV xv; arranges treaty, IV xv 6–9; letter to senate and Roman people, V i; imitates Marcus, V ii 3–4; alienates soldiers, V ii 3, 5, 6; sends Julianus to crush Elagabalus, V iv 2; defeated by Elagabalus, V iv 5–11; killed, V iv 11–12, v 2

Maecenas, VII xi 3

Maesa, sister of Julia: ordered by Macrinus to return to Phoenicia, V iii 2; daughters, V iii 3, 10, vii 2, 3; uses wealth to make Elagabalus emperor, V iii 11–12, iv 1–2; Elagabalus ignores her advice, V v 5–6; her grandson S. Alexander appointed Caesar, V vii 1–6; protects S. Alexander from plots of Elagabalus, V viii 3; rules with advisory council, VI i 1–4; dies, VI i 4

Magnus: accused of plot against Maximinus, VII i 4–8

Mamaea, mother of S. Alexander: trains son, V vii 5, viii 2, 10; bribes praetorians to support son, V viii 3; rules with advisory council, VI i 1–4; controls son after Maesa's death, VI i 5–6; greed, VI i 8; exiles son's wife, VI i 9–10; keeps son from battle, VI v 8–9; killed by Maximinus, VI ix 6–8

Marcia, mistress of Commodus: plots to kill Commodus, I xvi, xvii; selects Pertinax as emperor, II i 3–10

Marcus Aurelius: children, I ii 1, 2, viii 3, IV vi 3; character of, I ii 3–4; visits Pannonia, I iii 1; German tribes cause concern, I iii 5; farewell speech, I iv 2–8; plot against son-in-law, IV v 6

Martialis: persuaded by Macrinus to kill Caracalla, IV xiii

Materianus: assembles diviners for Caracalla, IV xii 4–5; informs Caracalla of Macrinus' plot, IV xii 5–6, IV xiii 1

Maternus: plots against Commodus, I x; killed, I x 5–7

Maximinus: military career, VI viii 1–4, VII i 1; proclaimed emperor, VI viii 5–8; kills S. Alexander, VI ix; savage rule, VII i 1–5, 12, iii, x 1; plot of Magnus crushed, VII i 4–8; defeats Germans, VII ii 6–9; revolt in Africa, VII iv, v; assassination rumored, VII vi 9; civil war in Rome, VII vii 1–4, x 5–7, xi, xii; senate leads revolt against, VII vii 4–5; speech to army, VII viii 4–8; march toward Rome, VII viii 9–11; Capelianus restores Africa to him, VII ix; enters Italy with army, VII xii 8, VIII i 2; siege of Aquileia, VIII iii, iv, v; killed, VIII v 8–9, vi 2, 5, 6

INDEX

Maximus [Pupienus]: urban prefect, VII x 4, 6; proclaimed emperor with Balbinus, VII x 3–5; character, VII x 4; appoints Gordian III Caesar, VII x 5–9; attacks Maximinus, VII xii 1–2; levies troops in Ravenna, VIII vi 5–6; informed of Maximinus' death, VIII vi 6–7; welcomed at Aquileia, VIII vii 2–3; speech to army, VIII vii 4–6; joint rule with Balbinus, VIII vii 8, viii 1; rivalry, VIII viii 4–5; killed by praetorians, VIII viii 3–8
Meniphilus, VIII ii 5
Moroccans: character of, III iii 4–5; javelin men, I xv 2, IV xv 1, VI vii 8, VII ix 1, 6, 7
Mysteries, III viii 10

Narcissus: kills Commodus, I xvii 11
Niger: career, II vii 3–5; plots for empire, II vii 6–8, viii 1–5; proclaimed emperor, II viii 6; Syrians scorned by Severus, II x 6–9; at war with Severus, III i, ii 2, 3, 9–10, iii; punishes defection of Laodicea and Tyre, III iii 3–5; defeated, III iii 3, iv 1–5; killed at Antioch, III iv 6
Numidians. *See* Moroccans.

Osroenians: king of, III ix 2; assassinate Quartinus, VII i 9–10

Parthians: character of, IV xi 3–4; deceived by Caracalla, IV xi 5–8, xiv 1; peace treaty, V i 4; attacks on, VI ii 6–7, v 6–7, vi 5. *See also* Artabanus.
Perennis: rise to power, I viii 1, 2; wealth, I viii 8; plots for empire, I ix 1–6; killed, I ix 6–10
Persia: methods of warfare, VI v 3–4, 9–10, vii 1. *See also* Artaxerxes.
Pertinax: adviser to Commodus, II i 4; proclaimed emperor, II i 5–10; accepted by people, II ii 1–4; praetorians forced to accept him, II ii 4–10; speech to senate, II iii 5–10; mild rule displeases praetorians, II iv 1–5; reforms, II iv 6–8; killed by praetorians, II v, vi 1–2, ix 8, xiii 1, xiv 3, VIII viii 2
Phadilla, sister of Commodus: warns of Cleander's plot, I xiii 1–4; killed by Caracalla, IV vi 3
Philocommodus, I xvii 3–4
Plague in Rome, I xii 1–2
Plautianus: daughter marries Caracalla, III x 5; rise to power, III x 6–7; plots against Severus, III xi, xii; killed, III xii 10–12
Pompeianus, brother-in-law of Commodus: urges continued war on Germans, I vi 4–7; marries Lucilla, I viii 3; devotion to Commodus, I viii 4
Portents, I xiv 1, 2, 6, II ix 3–6, VIII iii 7–8

Quadratus: plot to kill Commodus, I viii 4–8
Quartinus: proclaimed emperor, VII i 9; killed, VII i 10
Quintianus: plot to kill Commodus, I viii 5, 6

INDEX

Sabinus, VII vii 4

Saturninus: warns of plot against Severus, III xi 4-12, xii

Severus, Septimius: governor of Pannonia, II ix 2; character, II ix 2, 13, xiv 4, III v 6, vi 10, viii 3, 7-9; favorable portents, II ix 3-6; speech to troops, II x 2-9; acclaimed emperor, II x 9; march to Rome, II xi 1-6, xii 1-2; accepted by Senate, II xii 3-7; cashiers praetorians, II xiii; speech to senate, II xiv 3; prepares to attack Niger, II xiv 5-7, xv 5; Albinus appointed Caesar, II xv 1-6, III vii 8; defeats Aemilianus, III ii 2, 3; holds children of Eastern governors as hostages, III ii 5, v 6; defeats Niger in Bithynia, III ii 9-10; invades Cappadocia, III iii; breaches Niger's defenses in Taurus Mountains, III iii 6-8; defeats Niger near Issus, III, iv 1-5; plots to remove Albinus, III v, vi 1-8; siege of Byzantium, III vi 9; defeats Albinus, III vi 10, vii 1-7; kills Albinus' friends, III viii 1-2, 6; corrupts soldiers, III viii 4-5; stages shows in Rome, III viii 9-10, x 2; admits sons to imperial rule, III ix 1; invades East, III ix 1; siege of Hatra, III ix 3-7; attacks Parthia, III ix 8-12; escapes plot of Plautianus, III xi, xii; tries to reconcile sons, III xiii 3-6; expedition to Britain, III xiv; death, III xv 1-2; eulogy of, and final rites, III xv 2-3, 7, IV ii

Severus Alexander (Alexianus): adopted as Caesar by Elagabalus, V vii 1-6; reared by Mamaea, V vii 5, viii 10; escapes plots of Elagabalus, V viii 2-8; proclaimed emperor, V viii 10; his rule, VI i 1-4, 7; wife, VI i 9-10; excessive devotion to mother, VI i 10; war in East, VI ii; tries to appease Artaxerxes, VI ii 3-5; speech to army, VI iii 3-7; peace negotiations fail, VI iv 4-6; defeated by Artaxerxes, VI v 7-10, vi 5-6; threat of Germans ended through negotiation, VI vii 2-9; loses support of army, VI vii 10, VII i 6; killed by Maximinus, VI ix, VII i 3, 4, 9

Soaemias, mother of Elagabalus, V iii 3, viii 8-9

Sulpicianus, father-in-law of Pertinax, II vi 8-9

Syrians: character of, II vii 9-10, ix 6-7. *See also* Niger.

Thrace. *See* Byzantium.

Verus, Lucius, son-in-law of Marcus Aurelius: associate in empire, I viii 3; removal of, IV v 6

Vestal Virgins, I xi 4, xiv 5, IV vi 4, V vi 2

Vitalianus, VII vi 4-8, viii 6

Weapons, exotic, III ix 5, VIII iv 9-10

www.ingramcontent.com/pod-product-compliance
Lightning Source LLC
Chambersburg PA
CBHW021705230426
43668CB00008B/727